Learning Letters
Through All Five Senses

Formerly Titled: *Learning Through All Five Senses*

LEARNING LETTERS THROUGH ALL FIVE SENSES

A Language Development Activity Book

By Lois McCue   **Illustrations by Jula Libonn**

Gryphon House Inc.
Mt. Rainier, Maryland

©1983 by Lois McCue

ISBN 0-87659-106-3

Published by Gryphon House, Inc.,
3706 Otis Street,
Mt. Rainier, Maryland 20712

This book was previously published
under the title **Learning Through All
Five Senses**.

Design: Cynthia Fowler
Typesetting: Lithocomp

This book is dedicated to my grandchildren:

     Michael
     Amy
     Erica
     Tracy

It is also my pleasure to remember the many children who have inspired me in my teaching.

I would like to express special thanks to my daughter, Pam, who spent endless hours trying to decipher my handwriting and typing the manuscript. It is her express wish that I learn to type before embarking on my next book. Thank you, Pam.

Mom

Contents

Discovering, the child learns
Imagining, the child learns
Listening, the child learns
Creating, the child learns
Smelling, the child learns
Touching, the child learns
Playing, the child learns
Singing, the child learns
Dancing, the child learns
Walking, the child learns
Tasting, the child learns
Loving, the child learns
Living, the child learns
Moving, the child learns
Seeing, the child learns
Doing, the child learns

How do we teach young children? We let them imagine, touch, taste, love, and do. Even in our classrooms, we help children absorb life and knowledge through their own experiences. As teachers, we select and plan those experiences.

Children learn about the world, not through logic, but through their senses—their eyes, ears, noses, tongues, fingers. Over 300 years ago, John Amos Comenius described how children learned in his day, and it sounds like any pre-schooler you might meet in a classroom today:

"Those things, therefore, that are placed before the intelligence of the young, must be real things and not the shadow of things. I repeat, they must be *things;* and by the term I mean determinate, real, and useful things that can make an impression on the senses and on the imagination. But they can only make this impression when brought sufficiently near.

From this a golden rule for teachers may be derived. Everything should, as far as possible, be placed before the senses. Everything visible should be brought before the organs of sight, everything audible before that of hearing. Odors should be placed before the sense of smell, and things that are tastable and tangible before the sense of taste and of touch respectively. If an object can make an impression on several senses at once, it should be brought into contact with several . . . ." [1]

---

[1] George S. Morrison. *Early Childhood Education Today.* Columbus, Ohio; A. Bell & Howell Company, 1980.

In this book, the letters of the alphabet and their phonetic sounds are taught in a way that uses all of a child's senses. Most of us, including children, learn quickly with our eyes. When our learning also comes through our ears, we learn more quickly and remember more effectively. I feel children learn best when seeing and hearing are combined with the other senses in the learning situation.

By including all the senses, by letting children learn with their entire bodies, we can increase the richness of their awareness. We are laying the foundation for a lifetime of understanding the world in a way that is comprehensive. In learning the letter *P*, for example, see how varied the children's experience can be:

a. *p*ush an imaginary box over their head
b. smell *p*erfume
c. dance to a *p*olka
d. sing "*P*olly *P*ut the Kettle On"
f. mold "*P*" out of *p*lay-dough
g. read a story that starts with *P*
h. find something in the room that starts with *P*

That's a lot of *P* experiences, isn't it? Each of them could enrich a child's understanding of the world. We wouldn't use all of them in a given situation. We would choose activities that were right for a particular classroom of children.

You know children, so you know what excitement lessons like these will cause. When you open doors to nature, invite the children into science through experiments, let them experience the beauty of music and art, you teach them to reach out to the world.

As you use this book, remember education in the early years comes from living. Knowledge cannot be imparted from one to another, but experiences can be planned that require active participation that will help the absorption of that knowledge. Seeds of curiosity can be planted. Children won't retain all that has been taught in a given lesson or activity, but engrams (traces of the experience) will remain and surface in the future. Children are like sponges; they are capable of absorbing and retaining a vast amount of knowledge—and they do this best through the use of their senses.

In each experience, all of the senses, and motion, will be used. Each child should participate in at least one segment, but no child should feel he must participate in all of them. Be flexible and select the activities which you feel are right. Keep in mind that different children, as well as adults, learn best through different channels. A child who doesn't "get" an idea through sight and sound, may pick it up beautifully through motion or touch.

Because the experiences are free flowing, you can work with the children's individuality. There is no need for hurry, impatience, or harsh judgments. Pokey children can be free to poke; often it's the dawdlers who master and remember. The children can respond to you in groups, or one by one. Shy children and your sociable ones can learn side by side.

Although the experiences allow you and the children great freedom, their design is similar from session to session. This similarity offers security to the children—they know what to expect. They can look forward to being actively involved and challenged. Each experience should help your children develop and learn those skills which they must have later on, in order to read and write. I'm talking about skills such as effective listening, knowledge of environment, recognizing similarities and differences. The bibliography can help you draw up a list of developmental tasks you'd like to work on with the children. The tasks would be part of your underlying programmatic guide.

Each experience begins with a background explanation which may describe the materials you need or it may describe the developmental and educational tasks involved.

Before beginning, there are four things the children must know how to give and use: attention, courtesy, self-control, and respect for others. You can help them with these, by working in a circle. This makes the time special. As the lessons progress, the children's attention, courtesy, self-control, and respect for others will improve.

Having set up the ground rules that a child in the circle must show (attention, courtesy, self-control, and respect) you will introduce the experience. Then it is the child's time: time for active learning. This learning will take time and repetition. My six year old daughter used to pull her twin friends in a wagon up and down our hill, for days and days that stretched into weeks. She needed to repeat that task over and over again until she mastered it. When she was satisfied, she quit. Learning ideas also takes time and repetition, so give your students plenty of both.

To help with repetition and time, there are many activities for each letter. In all of the experiences you can let the children themselves select activities which will increase confidence, independence, and the ability to make judgments.

The experiences and follow-up activities in this book only scratch the surface. A teacher can employ the five senses and body movements to teach a concept in countless ways. It has been my intent to share this fundamental *method* of teaching, not to dictate lessons to other teachers. I want to share what has worked for me and been fun for children.

EDUCATIONAL BACKGROUND

Mystery Bag and the Sensorial Approach

The mystery bag is a small, attractive cloth bag that will excite and stimulate a child's curiosity. It is used to isolate the sense of touch from the other senses. It also instills respect for peers by "not telling" the mystery until everyone has had a chance to reach in the bag and identify the object for himself. Children love secrets and they love mysteries. This approach entertains and also sparks their interest for the lesson at hand.

Special Activity

A special activity is demonstrated by the teacher. During the demonstration be slow and deliberate in your movements. This will enable a child to follow and absorb the lesson being taught. It will also help her to remember the

sequence of the exercise when it is her turn to do it. These exercises are set out on a table or in a designated area for one child to use at a time.

When you present this type of activity you are teaching a child how to be patient and how to wait for his turn. You are helping him to develop a sense of trust because he quickly learns that if he does not have a chance to do the activity today it will be there tomorrow and the next day. A child's independence will blossom because of his ability to do an exercise without the teacher's help.

It is important when you set up these exercises to provide left to right directionality. Arrange the materials so that children are forced to work from left to right in order to follow the sequence of the exercise. This pattern of working will aid a child when she is learning to read.

Helpful Hints

Whenever dish detergent is used in an activity it should be diluted in order to avoid excessive sudsing. An eye dropper is a good dispenser for the detergent.

Aprons

An apron should be used in many activities. The apron protects a child's clothing from paints, water, food and many other messy materials. It also indirectly and subconsciously promotes a sense of neatness. The apron should always be returned to its proper place after the activity is completed.

MATERIALS NEEDED

1. Easel, alphabet card, label (animal)
2. Alligator in mystery bag, label (alligator)
3. Apples (sliced) in covered bowl, label (apple)

4. Song — "America", label (America)
5. Records (instrumental with varied tempos), label (action)
6. White vellum paper, apples, tray, paint, brush, knife, bowl, sponge
7. Paper
8. Pictures of birds and animals, label (animal), label (bird)
9. Basket of apples, apple slices, plate, pitcher, bowl, sponge, towel, cutting board, detergent, bucket

ATTENTION GETTER

Poem: *ANIMALS, JUST LIKE ME*

Boys and Girls
How would you like to be

an animal just like me?
I swing from branches on a tree
And people always laugh at me.
                                    What am I?

How would you like to be
an animal just like me?
I scamper here and scamper there
I gather nuts everywhere.
                                    What am I?

How would you like to be
an animal just like me?
I'm very frisky and like to bark
I get in trouble after dark.
                                    What am I?

How would you like to be
an animal just like me?
I roll in mud from toe and head
And never, never get sent to bed.
                                    What am I?

—Lois B. McCue

ACTIVITIES

1. *Alphabet card, easel, and label.*
   "Who knows what letter this is?" Discuss the short A sound. "Animal also makes A sound." (place animal label on easel) "Does anyone's name start with the letter A?" Ask someone to find A on the wall alphabet.

2. *Mystery bag and alligator.*
   Give each child a chance to say what he/she thinks is in the bag. Be dramatic when the alligator is taken from the bag. Explain alligator also starts with the A sound. (place alligator label on easel)

SPECIAL ACTIVITY: *Apple Prints*

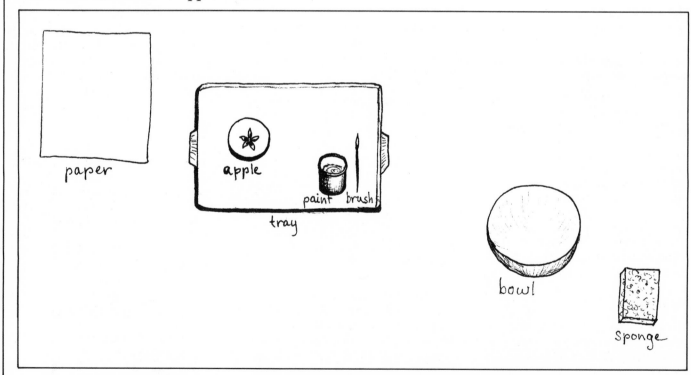

Materials: white vellum, apples, tray, paint, brush, knife, bowl, sponge

Cut apple in half (crossways), pointing out the star. Demonstrate how to paint the apple and print on paper.

3. *Apples, sliced in covered bowl.*
Explain that we are now going to smell something that starts with the *A* sound. (uncover bowl) Go around the circle and ask each child to close his eyes and smell what is in the bowl. (same idea as the mystery bag) Give everyone a turn to say what he thought it smelled like. (place apple label on easel) Give each child a piece of the apple to taste. Ask what sound the *A* makes.

4. *Song — "America"* (teach, if necessary).
Ask what letter America starts with. Ask what sound the *A* makes. Discuss the song and show America on the map. (place America label on easel)

5. *Action.*
Ask what action means and discuss the meaning. Ask for examples, (raising arms, moving legs, skipping, etc.) Ask what letter action starts with. (place action label on easel) Ask children to make the *A* sound. Record: Explain that they can dance to the music; this is also action. Remind them not to bump into the other children. Pantomime: Have children pantomime some actions. Remind them, pantomime is SILENT.

OPTIONAL FOLLOW-UP ACTIVITIES

1. *Take a trip to an apple orchard. Make applesauce.*

2. *Paper airplane.*
Demonstrate how to fold paper to make a simple airplane, then fly outside.

3. *Classifications.*
Two cards labeled "birds" and "animals". Collect nature stamps of birds and animals. Glue on poster board and laminate. (Note: the "birds" label is preparation for the *B* lesson.) Demonstrate how to classify in two sets: BIRDS, ANIMALS

SPECIAL ACTIVITY: *Apple cutting*

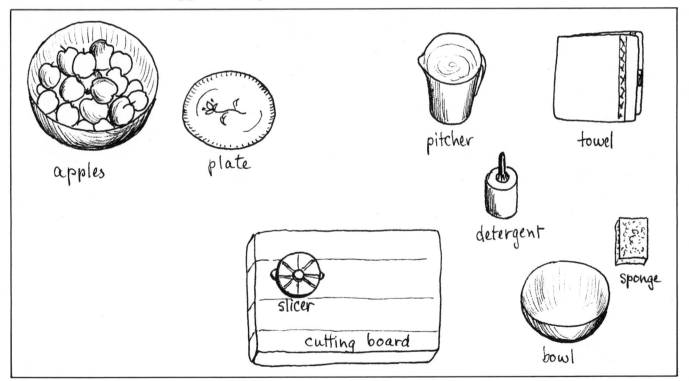

Materials: basket of apples (soft apples), apple slicer, plate, pitcher, bowl, sponge, towel, cutting board, detergent, bucket

Explain that the apples are already washed. Demonstrate: Place apple on cutting board and place slicer on apple. Press down. Remove core and put in empty bowl. Place apple slices on plate. Eat and pass out to children. Wash and dry plate. Use sponge to wipe table and cutting board. Empty water into bucket. Arrange table neatly.

Experience B

EDUCATIONAL BACKGROUND

Alphabet Card

Your alphabet cards can be hand made or purchased. Colorful alphabet cards with pictures appeal to children. All classroom visual aids should be at a child's eye level. Children very seldom look up and it's easier for them to see things at their level. Prefolded tape can be placed on the easel to attach each label as it is needed.

Alphabet cards help visual and auditory development. If the alphabet cards are textured, the tactile sense can also be employed. This activity seems to become repetitious as the lessons proceed, but the repetition is necessary for children's learning. The use of the written symbol combined with its spoken equivalent enables a child to integrate her visual and auditory senses. Children, as well as teacher, must voice the sounds in order to learn them.

Stories for Listening

The records and filmstrips used in *STORIES FOR LISTENING* (see "Materials") entertain while teaching. These lessons provide for the development of auditory and visual discrimination, imagination, creativity, concentration, social awareness and memory. These stories and filmstrips can be used for any lesson and can be used over and over. Children love and need repetition—repetition is a "security blanket." Louise B. Scott uses repetition in a way that captures a child's attention and concentration.

Button Vest

A button vest can be made or purchased. It's simply a vest, placed on a rigid frame, on which the child can practice buttoning.

MATERIALS NEEDED

1. Alphabet card—*B*
2. *STORIES FOR LISTENING* by Louise Binder Scott (filmstrip and record—*B*etty, *B*arbara and *B*ubbles
3. Box of crayons, manilla paper (12″ × 18″), and easel
4. Jar of water, straws, and strips of paper
5. Commercial bubbles
6. Bananas (one green, two yellow), knife, and mystery bag
7. Assorted bolts and nuts
8. Buttons or beads
9. Beads, string
10. Label (*bread*), ½ slices bread, butter, knife, placemat, plate, dish towel, pitcher with warm water, detergent, dish pan, sponge
11. Pictures of birds and animals. Label (*birds*), label (*animals*)
12. Jar, straws, sponge on tray
13. Button vest

ATTENTION GETTER

Nursery Rhymes:
Bye Baby Bunting
Little Boy Blue
Baa, Baa, Black Sheep

ACTIVITIES

1. *Alphabet card—B*
   Hold card and ask what letter it is. Discuss the sound. "Can you find the letter *B* on the wall alphabet?" "Does anyone's name start with the *B* sound? Do you know anything else that starts with *B*?"

2. *Filmstrip.*
   Continue with lesson until interest starts to fade.

Easel, crayons, and paper.
Draw bubbles on paper. (colors used in filmstrip) "What color is this bubble?" (repeat question for each bubble) Write the word bubble. Ask a child to point to a bubble that starts with the *B* sound.

4. *Jar of water and straws.*
   "Air can blow paper." Pass out strips of paper. Blow on paper. Ask what letter "blow" starts with. Write "blow." Explain that air is in our body, and that we can feel it if we blow into our hands. Pass out the straws and blow air through the straw into your cupped hand. Ask the children to do the same. Ex-

plain that air can create bubbles in water. Demonstrate by blowing into jar of water with straw. Encourage each child to take a turn.

5. *Commercial bubbles.*
   Take children outside to blow bubbles.

OPTIONAL FOLLOW-UP ACTIVITIES

1. *Bananas, mystery bag and knife.*
   Hold the bananas and ask children what they are and what letter they start with. Discuss the *B* and its sound.

SPECIAL ACTIVITY: *Spreading Butter on Bread*

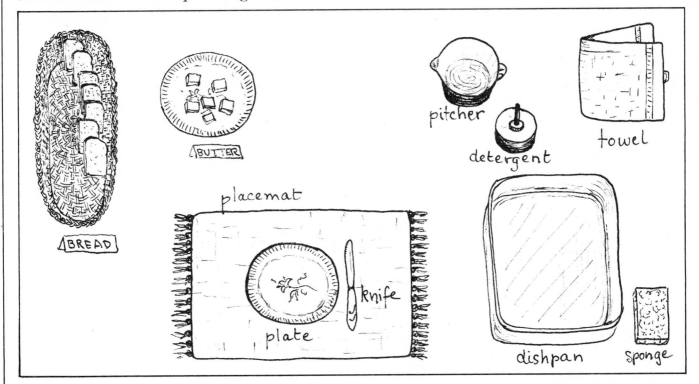

Materials: Label (*bread*), ½ slices bread, butter, knife, placemat, plate, dish towel, pitcher with warm water, detergent, dish pan, sponge.

This should be placed on a table to be used as a special activity and eaten by the child or shared with another child.

Pass the green banana around, then discuss the color, shape, firmness and smell. repeat the same procedure with the yellow banana. Then discuss the differences between the two.

Ask one child at a time to close his eyes while you place one banana in the mystery bag. Then ask that child to identify the color of the banana by touch or smell—or both if necessary.

Cut and give each child a piece to taste.

2. *Bolts and nuts to be assembled.*
These should be assorted sizes, unassembled, in a labeled container on shelf. Spend some time discussing how nuts and bolts are used, what they're made of, etc.

3. *Button or bead classification.*
This can be done by color, texture or size. They can be sorted using a muffin pan or a square of felt. You can discuss how they are used.

4. *Bead exercises.*
Stringing beads with or without copying perceptual pattern.

5. *Pictures (birds and animals) and labels (birds and animals).*
Have child classify.

6. *Jar, container of straws, and sponge on tray.*
Have child fill jar with water and blow bubbles with straw. Throw away straw and use sponge to dry the table and tray.

7. *Button vest on frame.*
This should be hung in classroom for child to use. Child can wear vest in room.

EDUCATIONAL BACKGROUND

Experience Paper

This is a large piece of paper on which you write words in heavy magic marker that come from the children during your discussion. The paper is on an easel which is the focal point of your circle. The atmosphere should be relaxed and intimate. Writing an isolated word or letter as you speak is effective with four and five year olds. You are integrating visual and auditory learning. As you go along, ask children to point out, comment upon, connect, or differentiate among words and symbols. This actively involves each of them. It provides the systematic drill children need in order to internalize concepts.

Rewards in Learning

It is recognized that external rewards should not be used in learning. The pleasure of learning should be the reward in itself. The introduction of this book points out that children learn best through their senses. Therefore it is appropriate that the children should identify and eat the cake that is discussed while learning about the letter *C*. The real cake involves the senses far more effectively than a make believe cake. The reward in this experience is the children's total involvement in a fun activity while learning a concept, not eating a piece of cake.

MATERIALS NEEDED

1. Easel, magic markers, experience paper, and alphabet card—*C*
2. Can (cake inside) and candle
3. Knife, plates, napkins, candle, match
4. Cardboard patterns for cat, cow & camel
5. Tray, scissors, crayon, glue, paper
6. Tiny objects that start with *C* (6 cards, 8 cats, 4 caps, 5 candles, etc.)
7. Poster paints, brushes, paper, sponge, tray

ACTIVITIES

1. *Easel, crayon, experience paper, alphabet card.*
   Write a large capital *C* on paper. "What letter is this?" Hold up alphabet card. Discuss the hard *C* sound. "Does anyone's name start with *C*" (if so, write on experience paper) Ask a child if she can find the *C* on the wall alphabet. Try to elicit *C* words: for instance, *cake, crawl, candle, car.* Put on paper. Make up stories with these words with children.

2. *Can with cake inside.*
   Hold can. "Does anyone know what this is?" "What letter

does can start with?'' Use crayon to write on experience paper.

"What is inside the can?" Give clues: "It starts with a *C*."
"We can eat it."
"It is sweet." (give them time to guess)
"We always have one at a birthday party."
"What letter does *cake* start with?" Again, use crayon to write on experience paper.

"Let's pretend we are going to a birthday party far away. Do you know something that starts with *C* that can get us there?" (car) "Ooops, the car won't start. Let's crawl to the party. What letter does 'crawl' start with?" "Who do you know whose name starts with *C*? (hopefully someone in the group, if not the children will come up with a name) "Okay, let's crawl to the party."
"Here we are."

3. *Knife, plates, napkins, candle, and match.*
Put the candle on the cake. "What letter does *candle* start with?" (Again, use crayon to write on experience paper.) Light the candle. "Can you smell the candle burning?" Sing Happy Birthday. What letter does *cut* start with?" (write on experience paper) Pass out the cake. While the children are eating the cake, read the words on the experience paper. "What do all of these words start with?" Ask each child to say the *C* sound.

OPTIONAL FOLLOW-UP ACTIVITIES

1. *Cutting.*
Label cardboard patterns—cat, cow, camel. Place on a tray with scissors, crayon, glue and paper. Demonstrate how to trace, color, and cut pattern. Demonstrate gluing on large piece of paper and writing word by the animal.

2. *Counting activity.*
Materials: Tiny objects that start with letter *C* (6 cars, 8 cats, 4 caps, 5 candles, etc.) Have children sort and count. Discuss letter *C*. The names of objects can be printed and a blank space left for the number.

3. *Poster paints.*
Demonstrate primary and secondary colors:

red painted on
yellow = orange
blue painted on red = purple
blue painted on
yellow = green

Ask what letter *color* starts with and what sound it makes. This can also be done with food colors. You might discuss how paints are made. Make clean-up (starts with *C*!) an integral part of this lesson. As children work, you might talk about the different kinds of cleaning jobs, and who does them.

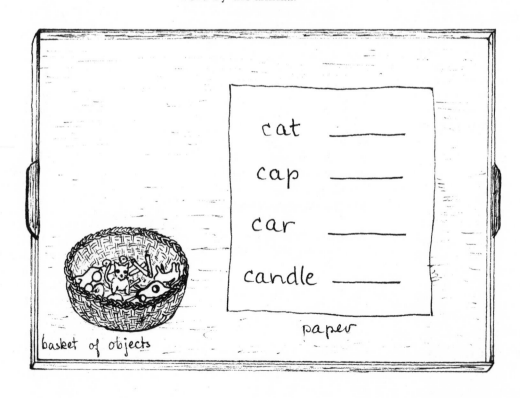

basket of objects

cat _____
cap _____
car _____
candle _____

paper

EDUCATIONAL BACKGROUND

Learning Through Play

Playing is learning. Children learn faster when they share ideas during play. The interaction that takes place between children while playing with puppets or dress-up clothes is a form of creative problem solving. One child may think of an idea and another will latch on to it. They will play for awhile, quarrel and then resolve the problem that they created. It is child's play, but they are practicing the social skills they need.

You, the teacher, must provide activities that welcome all kinds of pretend and make believe play. Blocks are excellent for math, language, balance and creative construction. Children will build and talk about bridges, tunnels, imaginary places and people. As children play they will learn to give and take. Children who learn to communicate and solve prob-

lems during play will feel free to solve problems in real life.

Dress-up Corner

A wide variety of clothes should be made available for children to dress-up in and pretend that they are someone else. It is fun and beneficial for children and helps them to have a better understanding of themselves. The clothing should be clean and orderly. Everything should have its place. The responsibility of caring for clothing during play will carry over to real life situations.

Puppets

Puppets are probably the most effective tool that a teacher has in an early childhood or kindergarten program. Children know that puppets are make believe but they love pretense. Puppets challenge children to respond to whatever situation is being presented. They entertain but also can be a means

to channel attention in a learning experience. Puppets encourage the development of creative and dramatic play. They also widen a child's imagination and help her to explore her own feelings in a safe setting. Puppets should be an integral part of your program.

Children also like to make their own puppets. They can be made by cutting out a paper figure and gluing it to a popsicle stick. This type of puppet is very good because the children can make them without help, and they love to say, "I made it myself." More sophisticated puppets can be found in many craft or curriculum books.

MATERIALS NEEDED

1. Miniature cardboard door and frame (made from a box), black marker
2. Dump truck with objects starting with D—1 for each child (dog, donkey, diamond, doll, dish, deer, dime, domino, drum, duck, dollar, daisy)

3. Puppets (doll, donkey)
4. Dates and napkins
5. Book—title or character should start with the letter *D*
6. Records for dancing
7. Puppets, dump truck
8. Dish drainer, dish brush, sponge, soap (in squeeze bottle), towel, water, pitcher, bucket
9. Feather duster or dust cloth
10. Dress-up clothes
11. Donuts and drink

ATTENTION GETTER

Nursery Rhymes:
Ding Dong Bell
Diddle, Diddle Dumpling

Poem: DING, DONG, DING
(use bells or xylophone for bells)

Doorbells are ringing,
Doorbells are singing,

Ding, Dong, Ding.
Ding, Dong, Ding.

Can you hear them ringing?
Can you hear them singing?

Ding, Dong, Ding.
Ding, Dong, Ding.

—Karen J. and Lois B. McCue

(can be sung to the tune: "Frère Jacques")

ACTIVITIES

1. *Cardboard Door and Frame.* What is this?" Draw a doorbell on the door.
"Does anyone have a doorbell?" "Did anyone ever ring your doorbell?" "Who rings doorbells?" (paper boy, mail carrier, etc.)
"Door and doorbell start with this letter." Write *D* on door with black marker. "What sound does *D* make?"
"Does anyone's name start with the letter *D*?" Ask someone to find *D* on the wall alphabet.

If you have time, you and the children might make up a *D*

SPECIAL ACTIVITY: *Dishwashing*

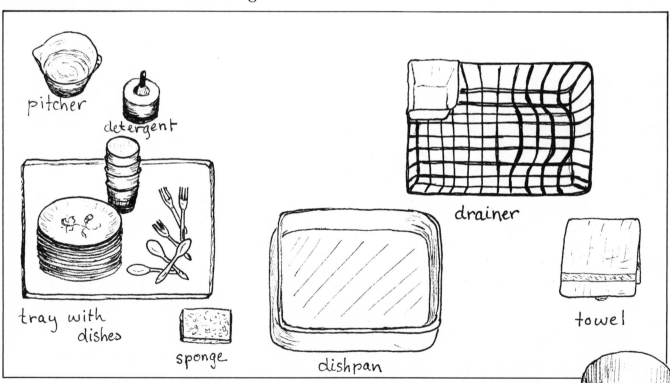

pitcher
detergent
tray with dishes
sponge
dishpan
drainer
towel
bucket

Dish drainer, dish brush, sponge, soap (in squeeze bottle), towel, water, pitcher, bucket

The teacher should demonstrate this activity and discuss the *D* words in the exercise. The pitcher has to be refilled by the teacher; the bucket is for the waste water.

story involving a door, and children whose names start with D.

2. *Introduce Puppet.*
"My name is Dolly. I live behind this door. My friend, Danny Donkey, lives with me. We like people to visit us. Will someone ring our doorbell?" (let children take turns.) *Note:* When the puppets answer the door, the questions and remarks can be either silly or serious. Make it fun. The first time you use dramatic play, the children may be shy. Give them plenty of time to relax with the experience.

3. *Dates and napkins.*
Dolly asks the children if they'd like a snack. A puppet holds up a dish of dates. Let puppet ask questions: "Who knows what these are?" (offer one to each child) The children may not have had dates. If this is the case, cut some in tiny pieces and encouraged them to try some. See who will *d*are to try a date!

5. *Book—a short story with pictures.*
Read and discuss. Point out words starting with D.

6. *Records for dancing.*
Ask the children what they can do with their bodies that start with D (dance). They may think of several activities. Let them name as many as they wish, then bring discussion back to dancing. Play the record and encourage children to dance. Encourage children to listen to the rhythm. Ask them to droop to the floor when music stops (demonstrate). Ask them to pantomime other D actions they think up.

OPTIONAL FOLLOW-UP ACTIVITIES

1. *Donkey and Doll Puppets, Dump Truck with "D" Objects.* These should be placed in an area for two children to play with as they wish.

2. *Dusting.*
A feather duster or dustcloth should be placed in the room (labeled) for children's use.

3. *Dress-Up Clothes.*
Clothes should be hung on hangers on a rack. This teaches order, encourages responsibility and fosters motor development. The D sound can also be disucssed.

4. *Doughnuts and Drink.*
The snack should be labeled to reinforce the letter sound. As you eat, discuss how doughnuts are made, and discuss the different kinds of doughnuts. Encourage children to say which kinds they do or don't like, and why.

Experience E

EDUCATIONAL BACKGROUND

Listening Skills

If we listed all the skills that help learning, careful listening would be right at the top. Listening helps children follow directions; it helps them hear the sounds they will see on the page when they read; it helps them gather information. Like any skill, listening can be improved with practice. Some classroom materials and activities sharpen listening skills.

Songs help children hear and use phonetic sounds, especially songs with nonsense syllables. They also convey information. Have your children listen to a song with a story, then ask them questions about what happened. You may need to play the record again to give children clues. You can put words from the song on an experience paper.

Hap Palmer's records use music to teach basic skills, including the complicated skill of following directions. Children enjoy being able to successfully follow his instructions. They immediately recognize their own ability to *listen* and *do*.

MATERIALS NEEDED

1. Flannel board and flannel-backed labels (exercise, elephant (Edgar), experiment, egg, empty, enter, and exit) and elephant puppet
2. Experiment: egg, 2 bowls, salt, 2 cups of water, ¼ cup of salt, and a spoon
3. Tunnel (small table covered with sheet) and two signs—*enter* and *exit*
4. *Record. LEARNING BASIC SKILLS THROUGH MUSIC,* Volume I "The Elephant" by Hap Palmer

Note: As you finish each activity in this lesson, put the flannel-backed label on the flannel board as you say the word.

ATTENTION GETTER

Sing or chant while doing various exercises (jump, twist, turn, etc.):

*"Exercise, exercise
Everybody needs to exercise."*

Poem: THE ELEPHANT
(hold picture of elephant)

*I'm an elephant, as you can see.
I'm big, as big, as big can be
My tail is short, my trunk is long.
My feet are big and my back is
    strong.*

—*Lois B. McCue*

ACTIVITIES

1. *Flannel board, elephant, and experiment.*
   "I'm an elephant and my name is Edgar, and I like to do experiments. I'll show you one with an egg."

22

Experiment:
1. Put 1 cup of water in each bowl
2. Put ¼ cup of salt in 1 bowl of water
3. Use spoon and place egg is fresh water
4. Remove egg and place in salt water

Results: Egg sinks in fresh water; it floats in salt water.

Let elephant ask questons, such as:

"What happened when the egg was in the fresh water?"
"What happened when the egg was in the salt water?"
"Where can you find fresh water?"
"Where can you find salt water?"
"Do they look the same?"
"Do they taste the same?"
"Do you want to taste the water (encourage each child to taste the water)
"Do they taste the same?"

2. *Tunnel.*
Elephant talking: "I'm tired of experiments. I want to make a tunnel." (fix the tunnel) "My tunnel is empty. I'm going to enter the tunnel; now it isn't empty. I'm tired and I want to leave. I'm going to exit from the tunnel."

Elephant asks questions, such as

"What does enter mean?"
"What does exit mean?"
"What does empty mean?"
"Do you want to enter the tunnel and exit the tunnel?"
(let each child have a turn)

Discuss labels on the tunnel. Let the elephant ask questions.

3. *Record.*
"Let's pretend we are elephants." Demonstrate. Play

SPECIAL ACTIVITY: *Egg Salad and Crackers*
For a group of one to three children.

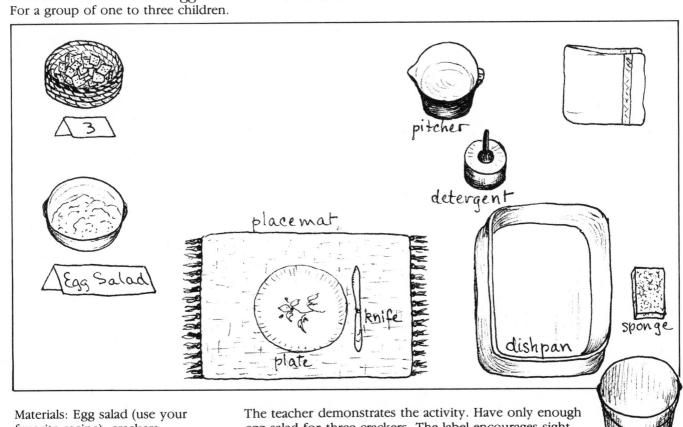

Materials: Egg salad (use your favorite recipe), crackers, placemat, plate, knife, pitcher, detergent, dishpan, sponge, bucket.

The teacher demonstrates the activity. Have only enough egg salad for three crackers. The label encourages sight reading. The dishes to be washed are the egg salad dish, knife, and plate. The table should be cleaned each time. The towel should be folded.

the record—"The Elephant" by Hap Palmer. Act out.

OPTIONAL FOLLOW-UP ACTIVITIES

1. *Elephant Puppet.*
   Materials placed on a special table for children to make their own elephant puppet. This would also have to be demonstrated by the teacher.

The children could be encouraged to name their own puppet (Eddie, Ellen, Egbert, etc.)

2. *Tunnel.*
   Put the tunnel in the book corner, or some convenient area, where the children can enter and exit in play.

3. *Egg Salad.*
   Boil eggs with the children.

Children can shell cooled eggs. (This is a good fine motor exercise)

4. *Clay.*
   Demonstrate how to mold an elephant. Have it lie down to support its weight. Allow elephant to dry for children to take home.

EDUCATIONAL BACKGROUND

Fingerplays

Fingerplays are an excellent way to gain attention or even to regain attention. All you need to do is start a familiar fingerplay in a firm but soft tone and children will immediately respond without further instructions on your part. Fingerplays create a relaxed atmosphere and are a terrific way to bridge the gap between activities.

In addition to being an excellent attention getter, fingerplays help to develop concentration, vocabulary, memory, finger and hand coordination and concepts such as math and identifying body parts.

Shelf Activity

It is frequently mentioned that materials and exercises are placed on trays or in baskets and then placed on a shelf. Children are given the freedom to choose an activity *and* the responsibility of cleaning it up. The opportunity to make these choices teaches children to care for materials and their environment. This freedom develops independence and self discipline.

MATERIALS NEEDED

1. Alphabet card *F*
2. Seven cards (labeled with the days of the week)
3. Easel, markers, and *party* picture. Drawing should include hats, ballons, presents, etc. Leave space in the picture for food.
4. Plates, napkins, and labeled food (hot dogs, fudge and figs)
5. Record—*CHILDREN'S DANCES WITHOUT PARTNERS,* "The Finger Game," by Lou Stallman
6. Flowers - any flowers that have a distinct fragrance
7. Finger paints, paper, clean-up materials
8. Pictures of faces with different expressions.
9. Mirror
10. Stamps, pads, and paper
11. Loose flowers, bottles or other containers (small flowers and spice bottles are popular), scissors, watering can

ATTENTION GETTER

Finger Play: *FINGERS, FINGERS*

Fingers, fingers,
Flit and fly.
Fingers, fingers,
Climb up high.
Fingers, fingers,
Turn and twist.
Fingers, fingers,
Make a fist.
Fingers, fingers
Crawl and creep.
Fingers, fingers,
Fast asleep.

-Author-source unkown

ACTIVITIES

1. *Alphabet card.*
   "What letter is this?" "Find it on the wall alphabet."

   Tell the story about how *F* got its sound:

   > "Once upon a time, there was a very happy cat sitting on a fence. She was purring. Pretty soon a dog came along and frightened the cat. The cat wanted to chase the dog away, so she went (make the F sound) because she was frightened. That is how the F got its sound."

   "What letter does finger start with?" "Is there anything else on our body that starts with the letter *F?*" *(fist, front, fanny, frown, face)*

2. *Seven cards.*
   "What day is today?" (lay out card on rug) "What day comes after today?" (lay out card on rug) Continue until all 7 days are laid out on rug. Ask a child to point out the day that starts with the letter *F*.

3. *Easel and party picture.*
   Ask children to identify the items in the picture. Ask what the items are for (party) Ask what is missing at this party.

   (food) Draw frankfurter and roll and ask "What is it?" (You could use a frankfurter, fudge, or figs, cut out of magazines instead) "Tell me another name for hot dog." Write frankfurter. Draw figs. Ask, "What is it?" Write figs.

4. *Paper plates, napkins, and labeled food.*
   Explain that we will taste the foods at this party. Pass out plates and napkins. Cut frankfurter into four pieces and pass out to children. "How many pieces did I cut?" "What does four start with?" "What does frankfurter start with?" "What sound does *F* make?" Pass out figs to children. "What does fig start with?" "What sound does *F* make?" Repeat with fudge.

5. *Record.*
   "What else do people do at parties?" (sing) Sing "Shoo Fly, Don't Bother Me."
   "What word starts with the letter *F* in the song?"

6. *Flowers.*
   Mention that people often have flowers at parties. Have children smell the flowers. Introduce the word "fragrance" and discuss the *F* sound.

OPTIONAL FOLLOW-UP ACTIVITIES

1. *Finger painting.*
   Encourage children to be expressive - let it be FUN! Maybe they could even print the letter *F* in the corner of the picture.

2. *Pictures and mirror.*
   Cut out pictures of faces with different facial expressions (happy, sad, crying, etc.) Ask what letter face starts with, what sound it makes. Ask children if they can make the same face. Place pictures and mirror on a tray for shelf activity.

3. *Fingerprints.*
   Place stamp pads and paper on a tray. Demonstrate how they can make their own fingerprints. Write fingerprint on paper and let children trace with pens.

4. *Flower Arrangements.*
   Place flowers and bottles on a tray, scissors and watering can on table. Demonstrate how flowers can be cut and arranged in bouquets. Water flowers. Ask children to place bouquets around the room. Discuss the *F* sound in flower and fragrance. Ask children to smell the fragrant flowers. Flowers can be field flowers or brought in by children.

EDUCATIONAL BACKGROUND

Seriation

Seriation is the ability to arrange objects, numbers, or words in a series—small to large, light to dark, etc. Objects like cubes, cylinders, nesting cups, etc. should be used for children's sensorial development. Maria Montessori's Pink Tower (cubes) and Brown Stair (prisms) are good aids for children's understanding of seriation. These items are graded in size from one to ten and can be ordered from educational catalogues.
The *THREE BILLY GOATS GRUFF* is a well loved story and is a good example of seriation.

Objects

Prepare a collection of small objects (charms, tiny toys, etc.) and alphabet letters or cards (with the printed letter on the card). The collection should represent the whole alphabet. Have a container with four assorted letters and three or four objects representing the initial sound of each letter. The letters should be placed on the left hand side of a mat, and then phonetically match the initial sound of the object to the letter.

Place mat, objects and labels on tray for independent play or work. Similar exercises can be made with the ending and middle sounds.

These exercises provide development for both auditory discrimination, visual perceptions, memory, organization, and good self concept.

Flannel Board

A flannel board is a large board on a stand which is covered with flannel. The purpose is to display flannel figures. These figures can be bought commercially: shapes can be cut from flannel, velour, etc; or pictures can be cut from magazines with felt pieces glued to the back of the picture.

The flannel board can be used to dramatize a story. It can improve a child's spoken language. Children must have the chance to verbally communicate with one another for more complex language development. When a child is able to talk and have people listen to what he is saying, he feels important.

MATERIALS NEEDED

1. Alphabet card, green marker, easel, and experience paper
2. Objects and labels (goose, goat, girl, gorilla)
3. Story cards: *THREE BILLY GOATS GRUFF,* by Louise Binder Scott
4. Goat's milk, paper cups

ACTIVITIES

1. *Alphabet card, marker, easel, and experience paper.*
    "What letter is this?" Write capital and lower case *G* with green marker. Discuss the

sound. "Whose name starts with the *G* sound?" "What color did I write *G* with?" "What letter does green start with?" Write green. "What do you see in the room that is green?" "What do you see in the room that starts with the *G* sound?"

"How many girls are in our circle?" Ask someone to count them. "How many boys are in our circle?" Ask someone to count them. "What makes the *G* sound - boys or girls?" Write both on experience paper after they answer. Underline girls.

2. *Objects and labels* (gorilla, goat, girl, goose).
Place objects on the rug one at a time and ask children to say the name of the objects.

3. *Story cards.*
Tell *THREE BILLY GOATS GRUFF* with story cards.

4. *Flannel board.*
Tell *THREE BILLY GOATS GRUFF* with flannel board. "What do goats like to eat?" Write grass.

5. *Goat's milk, paper cups.*
Talk about goat's milk/cow's milk. Ask each child if she would like to taste goat's milk. Ask what goat's milk starts with. Ask what sound does *G* make.

6. *Sing and dance - "Go In and Out the Window".*
"What does go start with?" "When I point to you, you may go in and out of the window."

OPTIONAL FOLLOW-UP ACTIVITIES

1. *Glue.*
Materials: glue, gold and green glitter, 2 labels (gold and green), 2 shallow pans, white vellum paper.

Demonstrate making a pattern of glue on paper by gently squeezing a small Elmer's glue bottle. Shake gold glitter into pan labeled gold. Repeat with green glitter. Discuss *G* sound.

2. *Flannel board.*
Flannel figures - *THREE BILLY GOATS GRUFF*. Place in area available to children.

3. *Seriation.*
Materials: pre-cut goats (small, medium, and large), precut grass, blue construction paper, glue.

Demonstrate how to arrange the goats on the grass from smallest to largest. Discuss the *G* sound in goats and grass.

4. *Morning snack - goat's milk and graham crackers.*
A child can serve his or her own snack when hungry, and it is the time designated for snack. Napkins, cups, crackers, and goat's milk should be placed on a shelf (in that order) with the labels under each item. The child first puts the napkin on the table, then the cup, the cracker, and finally pours the milk. This will reinforce the letter *G* and its phonetic sound and encourage independence. Once children know how to serve their own snacks, it can be done on a daily basis.

EDUCATIONAL BACKGROUND

Classification

Classification is grouping objects or ideas in a logical manner. Children's ability to classify begins in infancy. They can differentiate mommy from daddy, children from adults and animate objects from inanimate objects. They are not taught how to do this; it is an innate capability. The foundation for more complex classification has already been established.

We as teachers must take children from the known to the unknown: provide activities that will show likenesses and differences of color, shape, size, weight. The ability to see these relationships is necessary for problem solving in math and science.

Classifying objects shoud start with the concrete, such as hard and soft in the follow-up activities. Colors, shapes, and textures are also

good beginning points. Pictures of animals, furniture, flowers, hot and cold, are more sophisticated because they are abstract. Once children learn to classify objects, they can, and must, move on to classifying pictures, words, and ideas.

MATERIALS NEEDED

1. Alphabet card - *H*
2. Story: *THREE LITTLE PIGS*
3. Objects and labels (hammer, hat, hippopotamus, horse)
4. Blindfold, 2 jars of water (1 hot and 1 cold)
5. Hard and soft items, labels (hard and soft), three baskets (one labeled *hard,* one labeled *soft,* one filled with mixed hard and soft items)
   Hard items: stone, block, bead, etc.
   Soft items: cotton, fur, sponge, etc.
6. Tree stump, hammer, nails
7. Honey and wheat bread
8. Flannel Board: *THREE LITTLE PIGS*
9. Halloween items
10. Pictures of hot/cold items

ACTIVITIES

1. *Alphabet card.*
   "Who knows the story about the three little pigs?" "Can you tell me the story?" Show the children the letter *H* and discuss the sound. Let them make the *H* sound. "That is the same sound that the wolf made."

2. *Story.*
   Read the story - *THREE LITTLE PIGS.* Let the children huff and puff to blow the house down.

3. *Objects and labels.*
   Discuss objects and labels (see Experience G, Educational Background)

4. *Game.*
   Materials: Blindfold, jars of water (1 hot and 1 cold). Each child

should be given a turn to feel (blindfolded) the two jars of water and identify the hot one.

5. *"What can we do with our body that starts with the H sound?"*

"Yes, we can huff." Give clues for words:

Hold - make believe hold a baby or kitten

Hug - hug the friend next to you

Help - ask how we can help somebody

Hammer - make believe hammer

Hum - hum familiar songs and let them guess what song it is. Let children choose some songs that they would like to hum.

Hop - everybody hop around the room (first on the right foot, then on the left foot)

"Who can make an *H* on the floor with your body?" (Ask for three volunteers.) Do this a couple of times if all children want a turn.

6. *Sing.*
Any songs that have a word in the title that starts with the letter *H,* such as:
"Johnny Pounds With One Hammer"
"Ha, Ha This-A-Way"
Then, ask as you sing each song: "What words starts with *H* in this song?" "When I call your name, you may hop around the room."

7. *Hammering.*
Materials: tree stump, hammer (labeled), nails. This activity should be placed in an area for *one* child to use.

OPTIONAL FOLLOW-UP ACTIVITIES

1. *Hopscotch.*
Tape hopscotch pattern in the play area. Help children at first. Encourage boys to play. This is good for both muscular and social development.

2. *Honey on wheat bread.*
Spread honey on bread. Present differnt kinds of honey (clover, orange blossom) to talk about the different aromas.

3. *Flannel board play.*
THREE LITTLE PIGS

4. *Halloween activities* (seasonal).
Take advantage of holidays for language development.

5. *Hot/cold classification.*
Find pictures of opposites, such as:
cup of hot coffee - glass of milk
stove - refrigerator
sun - ice
soup - salad

Print two labels (hot and cold) and demonstrate how to place pictures.

EDUCATIONAL BACKGROUND

Movement and Learning

Children experience the world through their bodies. By dancing and moving freely they are learning to control their bodies in cooperation with their classmates. They are given the opportunity to learn about rhythm, pacing and distance, and creative movement. Frederick Froebel, father of the kindergarten, wrote "What a child imitates, he(she) begins to understand. Let him represent the flying of birds and he enters partially into the life of the birds. Let him imitate the rapid motion of fishes in the water and his sympathy with fishes is quickened. . . – In a word let him reflect in his play the varied aspects of life and his thoughts will begin to grapple with their significance."[2]

2 Tom Glazer. *Do Your Ears Hang Low?* Garden City, New York: Doubleday and Co., Inc. 1980, p. 1.

It is important that dance sessions should includ time for free expressive dancing where children can just be themselves. They will let go of emotions and become involved in the music. Without words, they will learn about their bodies and the world around them.

MATERIALS NEEDED

1. Alphabet card, experience paper, black marker
2. Incense and burner or dish
3. Rubber iguana (can be found in toy store), two labels ("inside" and "outside"), box
4. Pictures of an iguana and ibex (*NATIONAL GEOGRAPHIC* is a good source)
5. Inkpad
6. Large box (labels "inside" and "outside") and empty shaker
7. Song: "Go In And Out The Window"
8. Records: rumba, waltz, jazz, polka
9. Record: *IT'S ACTION TIME*

LET'S MOVE by Henry Buzz Glass

ATTENTION GETTER

Song: *I TISKET, I TASKET*

*I tisket, I tasket
A green and yellow basket
I sent a letter to my friend
And on the way I lost it.*

*I dropped it, I dropped it
And on the way I dropped it
A little boy, he came along
and put it in his pocket.*

ACTIVITIES

1. *Alphabet card, experience paper and marker.*
   Show alphabet card and discuss the letter and the *I* sound. "Find *I* on the wall alphabet." "Does anyone's name start with *I*?" Write the letter *I* on the experience paper.

2. *Incense and dish or burner.*
   Burn incense. Say and write the

31

word. "What letter does incense start with?" "What do you see?" "What do you smell?" Discuss the use of incense and the particular fragrance that you are burning.

3. *Rubber iguana in box and two labels, and pictures of iguana and ibex.*
Shake box. "What is in the box? Can you gues?"

"What letter does inside start with?" Write *inside* on experience paper.

Ask, "Is it hard or soft?" "How can you tell?" Open the box. Show them the iguana, say its name and pass it around the circle. While the children are looking at it write iguana on the experience paper. Ask what letter iguana starts with.

Show and discuss the labels *inside* and *outside*. Ask which one says *inside*. Tape *inside* label in box and *outside* label on the outside of the box. Show pictures of iguana and tape or glue on experience paper next to the word *iguana*. Discuss iguana,

where it lives, what it eats, and mention that it is a descendent of the dinosaurs.

Show pictures of the ibex. Ask what letter *ibex* starts with Write *ibex* on experience paper. Glue or tape picture on experience paper. Discuss ibex (same as iguana).

OPTIONAL FOLLOW—UP ACTIVITIES

1. *Inkpad, stamps and vellum paper.*
Discuss the word *inkpad* and what an inkpad is used for. Ask what letter it starts with. Demonstrate how to use the stamps and pad. Also demonstrate how to make finger prints and point out that everyone's fingerprints are different. Set up an activity and have children make their fingerprints to take home.

2. *Large box* (large enough for children to climb in and out of). Place box in an area for children to use. Discuss the labels *inside* and *outside* and glue onto the box.

3. *Song* "Go In And Out The Window"
Discuss going *in* and the letter *I*.

4. *Imagination.*
Select records with music that is native to certain areas or cultures, for instance the polka and Poland, jazz and New Orleans or the waltz and Europe. Select a record and talk about the people and place that the music originates from. Children love to use their imagination. Introduce the word imagine and talk about the letter *I*.

Ask the children to close their eyes and imagine that they are traveling to whatever country you were discussing. Tell them when the music starts to open their eyes and dance to the music.

5. *Record - IT'S ACTION TIME - LETS MOVE.* by Henry "Buzz" Glass
Follow directions for *Imagination.* (optional activity, #4.) Discuss *I* sound.

EDUCATIONAL BACKGROUND

Sequences

In learning sequence, children learn to follow a pattern. In the jeep exercise, for instance, the children follow a pattern they can see and do. To get it right, they must remember and imitate the proper order.

A story is a sequence: each event has its place in the order of telling. Children can recall a story you have just told them, as you ask, "and what happened next?" Or, they could pantomime the story.

There are cards you can buy, or make, that children can arrange to show a sequence. These cards might show a familiar story, or they might show a familiar activity, like baking cookies.

MATERIALS NEEDED

1. Alphabet card *J*
2. Objects and labels (jeep, jar, jug, jack-o-lantern)
3. *STORIES FOR LISTENING*, by Louise Binder Scott (Filmstrip "Old Jeremy and the Jeep")
4. Jelly and juice, plastic spoons, and a blindfold
5. Pre-cut jeep parts—body, tires, steering wheel, paper, glue, pencil
6. Jelly or jam on wheat bread

ATTENTION GETTER

Nursery Rhymes:
Jack and Jill
Jack Spratt
Jack Be Nimble

ACTIVITIES

1. *Alphabet card.*
"What letter is this?" "What sound does it make?" "Do we know anyone's name that starts with the *J* sound?" "Find the letter *J* on the wall alphabet."

2. *Objects*
Present objects (jeep, jar, jug, jack-o-latern). "Can you think of anything else that starts with the *J* sound?"

3. *Filmstrip.*
Explain that this story is about a man called Jeremy and his jeep - just like this jeep (show jeep). Show filmstrip and ask questions until interest starts to fade.

4. *Juice and jelly.*
"What is this?" (jelly) "What is this?" (juice) "What letter do juice and jelly start with?" "What sound does make?"

"How can you tell one is juice and one is jelly?" (see it) "What if you couldn't see it? How else could you tell what they are? (taste) "Let's see if you can. Here is a blindfold. Who wants to try?" Let each child have a turn.

OPTIONAL FOLLOW-UP ACTIVITIES

1. *Singing.*
"Let's sing songs that start with

the *J* sound." Songs: "Jim
Along, Josie"
"Jacob's Ladder"

2. *Jumping.*
"Jump also starts with the *J*
sound." "When I call your
name, jump."

3. *Activity #4* could be done again;
this time have children smell instead of taste the difference.

4. *Jumping*
(a) high water - low water (two
teachers hold ends of a rope
for children to jump over -
keep raising the level of the
"water")
(b) broad jump
(c) Jumping over cracks in
sidewalk

The *J* sound should be discussed for
each activity.

SPECIAL ACTIVITY: *Jeep exercise*

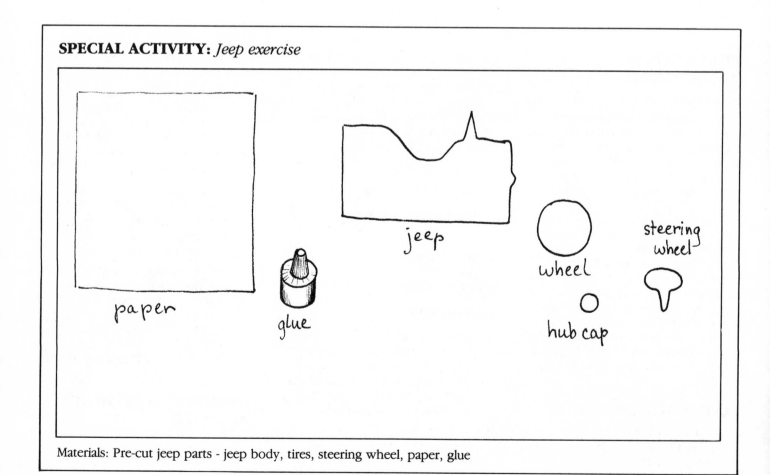

Materials: Pre-cut jeep parts - jeep body, tires, steering wheel, paper, glue

Jeep Pattern

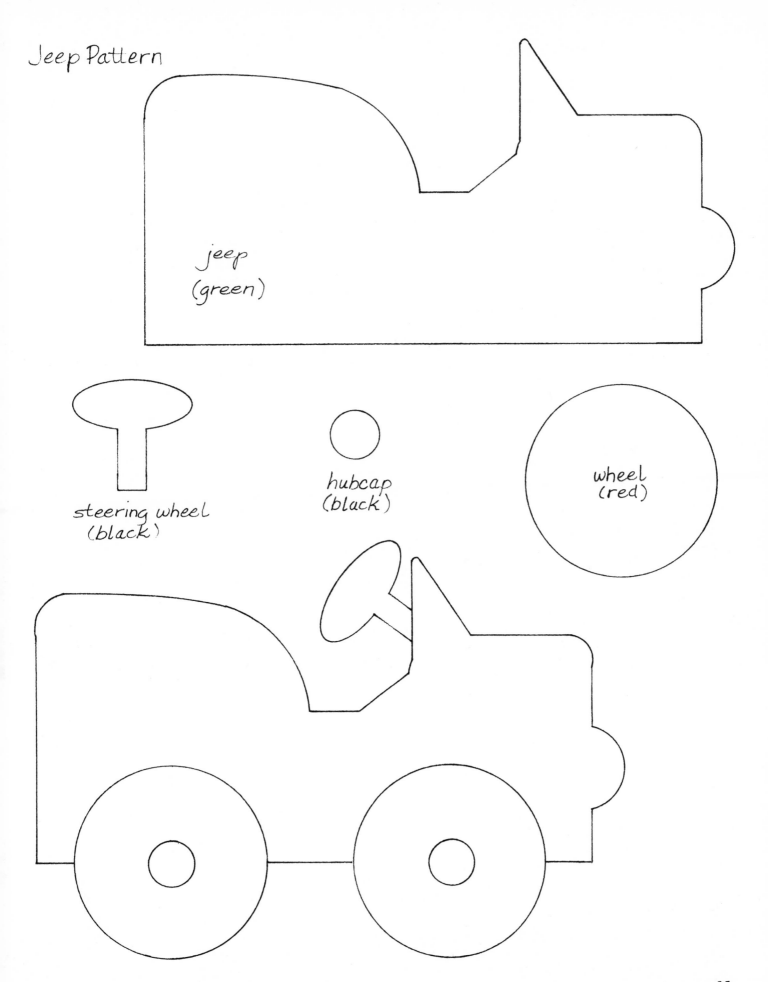

jeep
(green)

steering wheel
(black)

hubcap
(black)

wheel
(red)

Experience K

EDUCATIONAL BACKGROUND

Concentration

The art of concentration is a skill and must be practiced as any other skill. Prepare the children to pay attention by grouping them in a circle when you want to present a new activity. This will help to block out distractions. Special activities help to boost children's concentration because the nature of the activity *is special*. The children learn to understand that these activities are usually in the classroom for only a week, therefore they want to pay attention to what is going to happen. Special activities should be used as a tool to help children learn to concentrate.

Louise Binder Scott's *STORIES FOR LISTENING* are designed to improve listening skills and concentration. Play the story and show the film strip only once, then begin the interesting follow-up activities. By doing it only once children will learn to pay attention and concentrate.

MATERIALS NEEDED

1. Alphabet card *K*
2. Sandpaper letter *K*
3. Objects (kangaroo, kitten, kite) and label *K*
4. *Book - THREE LITTLE KIT-TENS*
5. Locked suitcase with key, containing four sets of paper whiskers, four paper tails, and four sets of paper ears (1 set should be larger for Mommy cat) and tape

ATTENTION GETTER

Nursery Rhymes:
Old King Cole
Polly Put the Kettle On

ACTIVITIES

1. *Alphabet card.*
   "What letter is this?" "What sound does it make?" "Does anyone's name start with the letter *K*?"

   Ask someone to find the letter K on the wall alphabet. If the similarity between hard *C* and *K* comes up, explain that *C* and *K* sometimes make the same sound and move on.

2. *Sandpaper letter K.*
   Trace the letter *K* with two fingers; then let each child trace it also. (a child has more control with two fingers than one)

   Song: *Make a K in the air, in the air.*
   Make a K in the air, in the air.
   Make a tiny, tiny K
   Make a great big K
   Make a K in the air, in the air.
   (tune: "If You're Happy and You Know It.")

3. *Objects and label K.*
   Show label *K* and the objects. Ask children to identify each ob-

ject and to say its initial sound. Ask if they know anything else that starts with *K*.

4. *Book - THREE LITTLE KITTENS.*
   Read the familiar book. Discuss the book. Discuss *kitten* and the *K* sound.

5. *Locked suitcase and key -* (containing costumes)
   Be dramatic about the key fitting in the lock of the suitcase. Use element of surprise when opening suitcase and finding costumes. Ask what we can do with them. (have a play)

Let children act out the story *THREE LITTLE KITTENS.* Let all children pretend to be kittens and crawl to the play area.

6. *Real kitten* (or stuffed kitten), *kitten food.*
   Show kitten; let children touch and describe it, emphasizing being gentle. Discuss age, color, diet, habits, etc. of the kitten. Ask children to smell the kitten food. Ask what it smells like. Ask if it smells like our food. If possible, leave kitten in the room for further observation. (of course children should be reminded about being gentle)

OPTIONAL FOLLOW-UP ACTIVITIES

1. *Kitten costumes.*
   Special area for children to role play with kitten costumes.

2. *Kitten puppets.*
   Special area for children to role play with puppets - possibly a puppet theater.

3. *STORIES FOR LISTENING,* by Louise B. Scott
   ''Crickety-Cricket'' - follow instructions.

SPECIAL ACTIVITY: *Kitten pattern*

Materials: poster paints (blue and green), 9 × 12 white vellum paper, pre-cut kitten pattern, assorted construction paper (brown, grey, white, etc.)

Prefold vellum paper in half lengthwise - or draw line through center of paper. Demonstrate how to paint the bottom half of vellum green and the top half blue (to the line). While paint is drying, demonstrate how to trace and cut out kitten pattern and then glue on picture.

Tape divider is to separate materials. Marker is to draw face on kitten. Tray is to collect scraps from cutting.

Experience L

EDUCATIONAL BACKGROUND

Vocabulary

Children learn new words as their experience widens. They learn the names of new objects and they learn words to show subtle differences. Their enjoyment of the world increases as they acquire language to describe the world. Children learn more new words as pre-schoolers than at any other time in their lives.

A child who doesn't understand the words you use will tune you out. It's tricky, because if you are boring your children by talking down to them, they will also tune you out! Carefully introduce new words, and use them repeatedly.

Children's reading ability depends on their spoken language. Give your children a rich language world: teach them long and short words, funny and serious words, words for color, sight, taste, touch, and sound.

MATERIALS NEEDED

1. Alphabet card, experience paper, easel, and marker
2. Book - *THE LEVER,* by Harlan Wade
3. Seesaw (lever)
4. Lemons (a little lemon and a large lemon), knife, blindfold
5. Lemons, juicer, sugar, cups, pitcher, water, plastic spoons
6. Lemons (cut in half) tea cup and saucer, one-cup tea pot, two spoons, juice squeezer, water, sugar
7. Ruler, spool, small rock
8. Label *(listening table). cassettes, tapes, correlated books*
9. Labels *(liquid and solid).* Pictures of:
   (a) water, milk, soup, ocean, lake
   (b) rocks, trees, flowers, dishes, furniture
10. Lotto Game, tray labeled *Lotto*

ATTENTION GETTER

Nursery Rhymes:
Little Robin Redbreast
Little Tommy Tucker
Little Bo Peep
Little Miss Muffet
Little Boy Blue
Little Jack Horner

ACTIVITIES

Note: Write each word that is a "key" L word on the experience paper at the appropriate time. Say each letter as you write it. Encourage children to join in.

1. *Alphabet card, experience paper, easel, and marker.* Discuss the sound. "Look where I put my tongue when I make the L sound."

   Ask what was the same about the poems that were just said. Repeat the names of the poems if necessary.

"What sound does it make?"
"Does anyone's name start with the L sound?"

2. *Book - THE LEVER.*
"The name of this book is *THE LEVER.*" "*Lever* also starts with the letter L." Read book.

3. *Seesaw* (refer to as lever) *on playground.*
Prove that the lever really works. Ask two children (equal size) to stand up. Let child A lift child B. Note that child A can only lift child B a little bit. Now let child B sit on one end of the lever. Let child A lift child B

much higher. Repeat this until all children have had a turn. "What letter does lift start with?"
"What sound does L make?"

4. *Lemons.*
"Who is little in our circle?"
"How can we decide who is little?" (measure) Measure children and write how long they are.
"What sound does *long* start with?"

Hold up two lemons. (little and big) "What letter does *little* start with?" Cut in half and ask each child to smell it; cut slices to taste. "What does it taste like?"

"What sound does *lemon* start with?"

5. *Lemonade and paper cups.*
"We are going to make lemonade." Squeeze lemons and add water. Use plastic spoons and let children each have a taste. "How can we make it sweet instead of sour?" (by adding sugar) Add sugar. Use plastic spoons and taste again. "Is it still sour?" Pass out the cups and pour the lemonade. As children are drinking their lemonade, read the words written on the experience paper. Discuss lemonade being a liquid.

SPECIAL ACTIVITY: *Lemonade*

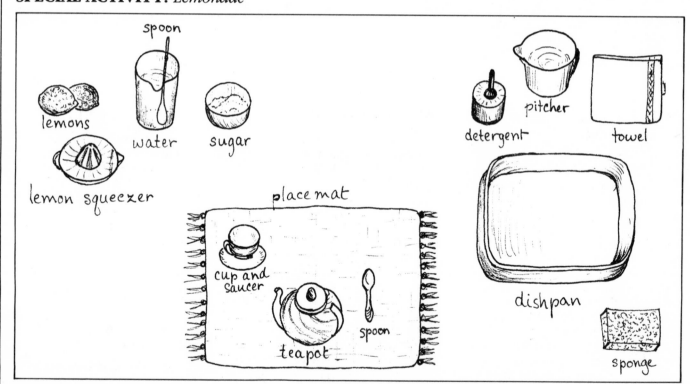

Materials: Lemons cut in half, tea cup and saucer, small one cup teapot two spoons, juice squeezer, water, sugar

Demonstrate how to make ½ cup of lemonade. Place tape on ½ cup line of measuring cup.
  (a) Measure mix into teapot.
  (b) Measure water and pour into teapot and stir.
  (c) Pour into tea cup and drink.
  (d) Wash and dry cup, saucer, and spoon.
  (e) Dry table with sponge.

OPTIONAL FOLLOW-UP ACTIVITIES

1. *Lever and Fulcrum.*
   Place on tray: Lever (taped ruler to cover number of lines), spool (fulcrum), small rock Demonstate how the lever works by using one finger. A piece of putty can be used to secure the fulcrum if desired. Discuss the letter *L*. Place on shelf to be available for children.

2. *Listening table.* (label *table*)
   Materials: cassettes, tapes, and correlated books Two children can share this activity.

3. *Classify pictures.*
   Labels (*liquids* and *solids*) and pictures of the following:

water	rocks
milk	trees
soup	flowers
ocean	dishes
lake	furniture

   Discuss the *L* and *S* sounds and classify pictures.

4. *Lotto game.*
   Teach game and emphasize the *L* sound. The tray on which the lotto game is placed should be labeled *Lotto*.

Experience M

EDUCATIONAL BACKGROUND

Memory and Retention

It is important that children learn to retain and recall information that they are exposed to. This skill can be developed. Children enjoy two and three part spoken directions. These can be fun exercises that are done in a gamelike fashion. Ask a child to touch his nose, hop around the table and sit down and have the others clap when he is finished. continue this game with varied directions until all of the children have had a turn. This game could be called the Memory Game.

Songs, fingerplays and nursery rhymes also improve a child's memory. *Concentration,* commonly called the matching game, helps children to develop a good memory. Some children need auditory stimulus to succeed at this game. Every child learns in a different way. Suggest to the children that they say

the name of the picture on a card as they turn it over. Suggestions such as this need not be verbalized if the teacher models the desired behavior.

MATERIALS NEEDED

1. Easel, markers, large piece of manila paper
2. Bread, cheese, plastic wrap, small tray, card labeled (*mold*), piece of moldy bread or cheese.
3. Record - music for movement (no lyrics)
4. *CITY MOUSE, COUNTRY MOUSE, COUNTRY MOUSE*—story
5. Basket with tiny muffins (covered), chef hat
6. *MICKY'S MAGNET* by Franklin M. Branley and Eleanor K. Vaugh.
   Tray with paper clips and a magnet.
7. Xylophone
8. Headset, tape recorder, songs to reinforce *M*
9. Muffins and milk
10. Matching picture cards, or post cards
11. *Concentration*

ATTENTION GETTER

1. *Easel, markers, manila paper.* Write large capital and small case *M* on paper. *"What letter is this?"* Talk about its sound. *"What am I writing with?"* (marker) *"Does anyone's name start with M?"*

2. *Bread, plastic wrap, small tray.* Ask if anyone knows what mold is. Pass around the moldy bread or cheese. While children are looking at it, explain mold. Tell the children we will try to make mold.

   Experiment: Wrap cheese in plastic wrap. Wrap bread in plastic wrap. Place on tray with label (*mold*). Tell children to observe the bread and cheese each day.

"What letter does *mold* start with?;; Write *mold*.

3. *Record - music for movement.* "Some music makes me want to sing and some makes me want to move." "What letter does *music* start with?" Write *music*. "What letter does *move* start with?" Write *move*.

"Let's move to the music without touching anyone." "We can move our fingers." "We can move our heads." "We can move our legs." (etc., etc.)

4. *Draw mountain on paper.* Ask children to identify what you are drawing. (if necessary, give clues) Ask what letter *mountain* starts with. Ask what sound *M* makes.

Sing: "The Bear Went Over the Mountain" (draw bear)

Story: "*CITY MOUSE, COUNTRY MOUSE*" Ask what letter *mouse* starts with. Ask what sound *M* makes. Ask which mouse would live by the mountain. (draw mouse) Ask questions about the story.

5. *Singing M songs.* Materials: basket of muffins,

chef's hat. Point out that the songs about to be sung have *M* words in them. Suggested songs: "Miss Mary Mack" "The Muffin Man"

Ask children to close their eyes and smell what is in the basket. (same idea as mystery bag) Ask what letter *muffin* starts with. Ask what sound *M* makes.

Ask someone to make believe he is the muffin man. (if possible, someone whose name starts with *M* - explain why) Have child wear the chef's hat and pass out the muffins. Write names of songs while children are eating muffins.

OPTIONAL FOLLOW-UP ACTIVITIES

1. *MICKY'S MAGNET.* By Franklin M. Branley and Eleanor K. Vaughn. This book explains to the reader and the children how to make a magnet. It is also a very interesting and fun book for children.

   A tray can be set up with a dish of paper clips and a magnet.

Demonstrate spilling the clips on the tray and picking them up with a magnet. Remeber to discuss the *M* sound and label *magnet* on the tray.

2. *Xylophone - to make music (not noise!)* This should be placed in a quiet area where one or two children can hear the notes and not disturb the other children.

3. *Headsets and tape recorder.* Tape music that reinforces the *M* sound. Example: "Miss Mary Mack"

4. *Muffins and milk for snack.* For one or two children at a time. Label the basket of muffins and the pitcher of milk.

5. *Matching picture cards of post cards.* Have two identical sets of cards. Lay one set on a rug and match the second set to the first set. Use the word *matching* discuss the *M* sound.

6. *Matching game (Concentration).* Demonstrate how to play.

Experience N

EDUCATIONAL BACKGROUND

Sensory Education

Maria Montessori suggested that we isolate children's senses when we want them to study a single sensation. For instance:

1. Obtain silence in the room and have eyes closed when listening for a particular sound

2. Blindfold children so they can feel differences in size, shape, or texture

3. Blindfold for the sense of taste or smell

4. Drawing in silence allows visual concentration

It would be beneficial for the teacher to be comfortable using the blindfold before she presents it to the children. This will help her to fully understand the sensations that will accompany the exercise.[3]

All of the senses are pathways to knowledge. Children, like adults, do not have the same strengths in all of their senses. Some can recall what they have heard better than what they have seen. Therefore it is important to present activities and experiences that will help to develop each sense to its fullest.

MATERIALS NEEDED

1. Alphabet card, easel, manila paper, markers
2. *STORIES FOR LISTENING,* "The Mysterious Sound," by Louise B. Scott
3. Markers
4. Identical bottles with scented cotton balls (peppermint, perfume, lemon, etc.)
5. Nurse (or nurse's uniform)
6. Nurse uniform and cap
7. Two hazel nuts. two peanuts, two walnuts, two brazil nuts, etc., basket, blindfold, mat
8. Paper squares, styrofoam packing chips, cut straws, assorted beads, plastic needle, yarn
9. Mixed nuts, nutcracker, two baskets, placemat, label *nuts*

ATTENTION GETTER

Number Song:
I know who can count to ten, *
Count to ten
Count to ten.
I know who can count to ten,
*And his name is ** _____*

(tune: "All Around the Mulberry Bush")

*Keep changing the number
**sing the name of a child here

ACTIVITIES

1. *Easel, paper, markers, alphabet card.*
   "What did we just sing about?" Hold up alphabet card. Discuss the letter *N* and the *N* sound.

---

[3]Oren, R.C. *A Montessori Handbook,* New York: Capricorn Books, 1966, pp. 102–103

Write the word *number*. "Does anyone's name start with *N*?" Write name.

2. *"The Mysterious Sound"*
   Follow directions.

3. *Markers.*
   Draw pictures: nurse, nail, necklace, nose, net, nine, needle, etc. As you draw each picture, ask children to identify it. Ask what letter it starts with. Write word under each picture. Ask children to say the letters as you write word. Ask what sound the first letter makes. Repeat process for each picture.

4. *Bottles with scented cotton balls.*
   Ask what our nose does. (smells) Pass bottles to children and ask them to use their noses (close eyes) to identify what they smell. Keep changing bottles to fool the children.

5. *Nurse.*
   Introduce the nurse by drawing a picture of a nurse and ask children to guess what you are drawing. Write *nurse* under the picture.

   Have a nurse visit and talk about his or her profession. (If a nurse is not available, a nurse's uniform could also be used.)

OPTIONAL FOLLOW-UP ACTIVITIES

1. *Nurse uniform and cap.*
   Place in dress up corner.

2. *Classification.* (two children)
   Materials: two hazel nuts, two peanuts, two walnuts, two brazil nuts, etc., basket, blindfold, mat. Place nuts in a basket with blindfold and mat. Lay nuts on mat and put on blindfold.

   Demonstrate:
   (a) Ask child to hand you one nut.
   (b) Hold nut in one hand and feel other nuts until you can match it through the sens of touch.
   (c) Set two matching nuts aside.
   (d) Repeat until all are matched.

3. *Necklace.*
   Materials: paper squares, styrofoam packing chips, cut straws, assorted beads, etc., plastic needle, yarn. Combine two or three items and thread on yarn with a plastic needle.

SPECIAL ACTIVITY: *Nuts*
For one or two children.

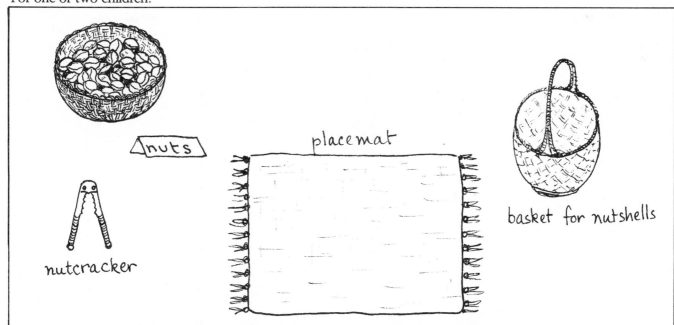

nuts

nutcracker

placemat

basket for nutshells

Materials: mixed nuts (almonds, peanuts, hazel nuts), nutcracker, baskets (two), placemat, label (nuts)

Demonstrate how to crack nuts and clean table.

Experience O

EDUCATIONAL BACKGROUND

Imagination

Children come to school and love to tell you stories. Some of these stories reflect a vivid imagination. Help them to explore their imagination by giving them the opportunity to complete open ended stories. Unfinished stories can be read to children or can be made up on the spur of a moment. They can be planned ahead of time by using props to create a setting for the story. Another method is to have a box of objects or toys and have a child reach in and select one, two or three things and create a story for the rest of the group. It can be a silly story or a serious story. Let the child's imagination decide. This could be a daily activity where a different child is chosen each day. When children are developing their imagination and verbal expression they are steadily increasing their vocabulary skills. These activities are fun and very rewarding.

Spatial Relationships

Experience #5 is a good example of how the whole body can be used to internalize a concept. The children start out by using fine muscle then large muscle activities. They then go even further by moving away from their own body and include the bodies of other children to learn about the letter O. A child is given the opportunity to make the O, see the O, feel the O, and be part of the O. It also gives him a very good idea of how he fits into his own space and the space around him. He is also given a pretty good idea of his relationship to others in that space.

MATERIALS NEEDED

1. Alphabet card, orange marker, experience paper
2. Mystery bag, octopus
3. Flannel board, flannel figures (octopus, orange, fish, shells, Oliver (boy), ocean waves)
4. Oranges and napkins in a bag
5. Flannel board and figures
6. Chalk board, orange chalk, label (*orange*)
7. Label (*orange*), oranges, orange juice, squeezer, glass pitcher, towel, detergent, dish pan, sponge

ATTENTION GETTER

Song: "Oh Dear, What Can the Matter Be?"

Book: Any book where attention can be focused on the letter O. (Such as *THE ONE MISSING PIECE MEETS THE BIG O,* by Shel Silverstein)

ACTIVITIES

1. *Alphabet card, orange marker, experience paper.*
   "What letter is this?" "Find the letter O on the wall alphabet."

Explain the short *O* sound. "Does anyone's name start with the letter *O*"

2. *Mystery bag, octopus.*
Let each child feel the octopus. Let children describe the octopus. Encourage them to give information about the octopus. "What letter does *octopus* start with?" "What sound does it make?"

3. *Flannel board, flannel figures.*
Start unfinished story: *"Once upon a time, there was an octopus that lived in the ocean (put octopus on flannel board), and he was lonely. . ."*

Name the other flannel figures and place on the flannel board away from the octopus. (These figures will be used as props for finishing the story) Ask the children to finish the story. Ask again what letter *octopus* starts with. "Does anything else in the story start with *O?*"

4. *Oranges and napkins in bag.*
Ask each child to smell what is in the bag. Show them the napkins; ask if this is what they smelled. Show them the orange; ask if this is what they smelled. Peel and pass out one section of the orange to each child. Discuss the taste, texture, etc.

5. *The O shape.*
"Can you make the *O* shape with your fingers?" "Can you make the *O* shape with your mouth?" "Can you make the *O* shape with your arms?" "Can you make the *O* shape with your body?" "Can two people make an *O?*"

"Let's stand up, hold hands, and make a big circle." "What letter does our circle look like?" Discuss the *O* sound.

Let one child at a time sit down (continue to hold hands); point out that the *O* is getting smaller and smaller. Ask if there is a part of their body that is *O* shaped (eyes)

6. *Flannel board.*
Individual or small group. Use flannel board figures to reenact the open ended story, or create a new one.

7. *Chalk board, orange chalk.*
These are to be used for creative expression. Tape label (orange) on upper left-hand corner.

SPECIAL ACTIVITY: *Make orange juice*

Materials: label (*orange*), oranges, orange juice squeezer, glass, pitcher, towel, detergent, dishpan, sponge

Demonstrate how to squeeze orange. Pour into glass. Point out the pulp-the smell - the color. Pour into glass and drink juice. Wash glass.

Experience P

EDUCATIONAL BACKGROUND

Painting

Poster painting, print painting, finger painting, or water colors not only give children the opportunity for creativity, but also help develop an understanding of primary and secondary colors. Painting provides the opportunity to appreciate a color and its different hues. It also helps to develop a sense of law and order and self-discipline. Painting aids in developing fine muscle control necessary for writing.

Children seem to have an inner drive to represent their world on paper. They want to represent their experience in that world on paper. This may go back to the caveman and his desire to paint pictures when he could not write. It seems to be innate and teachers should provide opportunities to release these desires and inner drives.

Children naturally love the brightness, the boldness, the challenge of painting. Some paints, like finger paints, even have a special smell. Painting integrates a child's perceptions of space, shape, color, feeling. Children can paint about their inner world, as well as the outer one. Through paint, they can discover subtle differences.

As a teaching tool, painting can teach eye-hand coordination, self-control and order, and it can help children make connections between their inner and outer worlds.

Puzzles

Puzzles can be used as a reinforcement for a letter and its sound. They also provide a basic foundation for math. It is a concrete demonstration that a whole is made up of many parts.

MATERIALS NEEDED

1. Alphabet card, purple marker, experience paper
2. Objects - pliers, pig, piano, pine cone, perfume, label *P*
3. Small present (peanuts) wrapped in large present
4. Unfinished story cards - "The Box," by Louise Binder Scott
5. Pink and purple paints in labeled jars, white vellum paper
6. Peanut butter and crackers
7. Pumpkins (trip to farm)
8. Ingredients for pumpkin pie (use favorite recipe) tart pans, rolling pin, floured place mat, two pitchers, plate, measuring cup, bowl and sponge

ATTENTION GETTER

Nursery Rhymes:
Peter, Peter, Pumpkin Eater
Peas Porrige Hot

Song: *"Pop Goes the Weasel"*

ACTIVITIES

1. *Alphabet card.*
   Song: *Make a P in the air, in the air*
   Make a P in the air, in the air
   Make a great big P,

Make a tiny, tiny P,
Make a P in the air, in the air.

(tune: "When You're Happy and You Know It")

"Can you find the letter *P* on the wall alphabet?"

2. *Objects*
Pliers, pig, piano, pine cone, perfume, label *P*. Have children say the names of the objects. Have children smell the pine cone and perfume. Have children repeat the names of the objects while holding their hands in front of their mouths. "Can you feel the air push out

of your mouth when you say the letter *P?*" Have the children make the *P* sound and again feel the air.

3. *Large present in a bag - small present in a large present.*
"What do you think is in this present?" "Isn't it beautiful? If this were your present, what would you like it to be?" (ask each child) "I'm going to pass it around and you try to guess what it is." Ask each child what he/she thinks it is.

Open the present. Be dramatic. Peek inside and close it quickly.

Keep peeking inside the present until the children ask to see it too.

"What did I do?" 'Do you want to peek inside too?" "What letter does *peek* start with?" Pass the present around again. Tell the children to "Peek inside, but don't tell what you see. It's a secret." After everyone has had a turn to peek (there is a lot of giggling by this time). Repeat procedure with small present - then share peanuts.

4. *Unfinished story cards.*

SPECIAL ACTIVITY: *Pumpkin pie*
For one person.

 pie crust balls
 pie filling
 measuring cup
 tart pans
 water

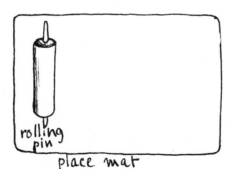 rolling pin place mat
 bowl
 sponge

Materials needed: Ingredients for pumpkin pie (use your favorite recipe), tart pans, rolling pin, floured place mat, two pitchers, plate, measuring cup, bowl and sponge.

Make filling and crust as a total group activity. Measure crust into small balls for tart pans. Pour filling into small pitcher (easier to handle) for children to pour into marked pitcher.

5. *Make believe present*
Have children stand up and hold a make believe present. Tell them that the present is very heavy and they must push it up over their heads and say "push." Strain while pushing so that the *P* in *push* is really emphasized.

"What else can we do that starts with the letter *P*. What do you like to play?"

6. *Poster painting.*
Use pink and purple paints (labeled jars) and white vellum paper. Encourage creative designs. Children can paint with bits of sponge, as well as with brushes. Large pieces of paper encourage experimentation.

7. *Peanut butter and crackers.*
Place an uncovered jar of peanut butter in a bag. Have children close their eyes and guess what it is by the smell. Use peanut butter and crackers for a special activity to be shared by one to three children.

8. *Pumpkin picking.*
If this lesson falls around Halloween, arrange for the children to visit a farm and pick pumpkins to paint for a jack-o-lantern

Discuss the *P* sound in *pick, pumpkin, and paint*. Alternatives: peas (in pods), peaches, potatoes, pears, parsley (could be grown in room)

Experience Q

EDUCATIONAL BACKGROUND

Fine Muscle Development

Zippering a jacket, buttoning a sweater, opening a door, and turning a water faucet on and off, require a child's fine motor skills. Many pre-school children are just getting started on these skills.

At school, children learn to cut, glue, paint, color, build with small objects, and even pour water from a pitcher. They will enjoy their success, and these skills will prepare them for later learning. Some of our children need to practice these skills over and over again. Be cheerful and encouraging: practice *does* make (almost) perfect!

Sand Paper Letters

You can buy sand paper letters, or make your own. To make your own, cut the alphabet letter out of sand paper and glue it onto a smooth board or sheet of poster board. Show the child how to trace the letter using two fingers, the pointer and middle ones. The child will use touch, sight, and even hearing to learn letters this way. The same method can be used with numbers.

MATERIALS NEEDED

1. Alphabet card, sand paper letter, flannel board, label (*quack*)
2. Objects—quarter, queen, piece of quartz, and labels for each word.
5. Puppets—mother duck and five babies
6. Paper (white vellum), paint (green and yellow), potato, jars, brushes, water pitcher, bowl, sponge

ATTENTION GETTER

Poem: *Quack Quack Song*
(hold duck puppet or toy duck)

Danny Duck is a friend of mine;
He quacks a tune all the time.
All day long, he quacks and swims;
Sometimes I even swim with him
But when I do it's not for long;
I get tired of his quack, quack song.

—Lois B. McCue

ACTIVITIES

1. *Alphabet card, sand paper letter, flannel board, label (quack)*
"What letter is this?" "Can someone find *Q* on the wall alphabet?" Discuss the sound. Mention that *quack* from our song starts with *Q*. Place label *quack* on the flannel board. Let each child trace sand paper letter.

2. *Objects.*
Place an object on the rug. Place the label on the flannel board. Repeat with each object.

3. Poem: *Five Little Ducks*
(fingerplay)

Five little ducks went swimming one day
Over in the pond and far away.

53

*Mother duck said, "Quack,
   quack, quack, quack,"
But only four little ducks came
   back.*

Four little ducks...

Three little ducks...

Two little ducks...

One little duck...

*Five little ducks came back one
   day
Over the pond and far away.
Mother duck said, "Quack,
   quack, quack, quack,"
As five little ducks came
   swimming back.*

   —Tom Glazer

(While reciting the poem "Five
Little Ducks," the left arm

makes a swimming motion while
right hand holds up five fingers.
Drop a finger on each verse.
Raise five fingers again on the
last verse.)

Six children could also act the
poem out in the center of the
large circle. It could be re-
peated until everyone has a
turn. Ask again what sound
quack starts with. "What sound
does the Q make?"

4. *Unfinished story.*
   Objects from activity #2. Use
   objects (queen, quartz, quarter)
   and start an open ended story:

   *Once upon a time, a duck was
   sitting on a piece of quartz. The
   duck was crying because...*

Encourage the children to finish
the story using the other objects. The story will undoubtedly
be short and more than one can
be told. Continue until interest
wanes. Reinforce the Q sound.

Children could also act out the
unfinished story with props.

OPTIONAL FOLLOW-UP ACTIVITIES

Puppets.
Use a mother duck puppet and five
baby duck puppets for this activity.
Place in area for role playing. Could
use stuffed animals instead.

SPECIAL ACTIVITY: *Potato print*

potato on tray

pencil in jar

pitcher with water

yellow paint

green paint

bowl

sponge

Materials: Paper (white vellum),
paint (green and yellow),
potato, jars, brushes, water
pitcher, bowl, sponge

Before the activity, teacher carves a simple duck outline on the flat surface of a peeled potato cut in half. Demonstrate painting grass on white
vellum (allow to dry). Paint carved potato duck yellow and stamp on
paper (on grass). Print quack, quack on paper with brush or markers. (If
child cannot print, teacher will print.) Use water, bowl, and sponge to
clean table.

Experience R

EDUCATIONAL BACKGROUND

Coordination and Motor Skills

Children are free to learn academics when they can handle their bodies with confidence and skill. To move vigorously and capably is as human as talking or laughing. Our children need to:

1. Run for endurance and strength

2. Throw for eye-hand coordination

3. Walk sideways, backwards, on a line or balance beam to develop balance

4. Jump from safe heights, over objects, over distances

5. Skip: this is difficult for young children. Give them time and tender, loving encouragement.

MATERIALS NEEDED

1. Alphabet card, easel, experience paper, and red marker

2. Rhyming cards—four sets (four cards in each set)

pan	can	man	fan
star	car	bar	jar
men	ten	hen	pen
cat	hat	rat	bat

3. Riddles—a selection of simple riddles

4. Rye bread—cut in two inch squares and keep in covered bowl, relish (in covered jar) and spoon

5. Races and taped roads

6. Games that start with the letter *R*

7. Book—*LITTLE RED RIDING HOOD*

8. Ring toss

9. Paints, crayons, or play dough

10. Bells in four graduated sizes

ATTENTION GETTER

Nursery Rhymes:
Rock-A-Bye Baby
Rub-A-Dub-Dub
Rain, Rain, Go Away
It's Raining, It's Pouring

ACTIVITIES

1. *Alphabet card, easel, experience paper, and red marker.*

   "What letter is this?" Write *R* on experience paper. "What color did I write *R* with?" Write *red*. "Whose name starts with the letter *R*?" Write name. "What sound does the letter *R* make?" Discuss the sound. "What letter does *red* start with?" Point to the word *red*. Ask someone to locate *R* on the wall alphabet.

2. *Rhyming cards.*
   Introduce cards and the word *rhyme*. Ask what letter *rhyme* starts with and write *rhyme*. Present the exercise with child participation.

   Rhyming Cards (pan, can, man, fan; star, car, jar, bar; men, ten, hen, pen; cat, hat, rat, bat) Talk about rhymes.

3. *Riddles.*
Introduce the word *riddle*. "What does *riddle* start with?" Write *riddle*.

Present riddles—2 examples:

Who lives in a house in a tree and hides her babies from you and me? (bird)

What is shiny and bright, lives in the sky and can be seen only at night? (moon)

4. *Rye bread and relish.*
Let each child close his/her eyes and smell the bread. After every child has had a turn, let them guess what they smelled. Write *rye bread*. Repeat activity with the relish. Offer rye bread and relish to each child to taste.

5. *Races.*
"Who knows what a race is?" "What letter does *race* start with?" Write *race*. "Who knows what a road is?" "What letter does *road* start with?" Write *road*.

Explain that we are going to have races on roads. Point out that they will all be races that start with the letter *R*.

Write the races on experience paper:

Running
Rolling (like logs or balls)
Rubbing (sliding—rubbing tummies on the road)

OPTIONAL FOLLOW-UP ACTIVITIES

1. *Games that start with the letter R.*
Example: "Ring Around the Rosie"

2. *Book—LITTLE RED RIDING HOOD*

3. *Rainbow.*
Children can make rainbows from:
(a) poster, finger, or water color paints
(b) crayons (paper removed); use on their sides
(c) play dough (bright colors); make into "snakes" and place in an arch close together. (good creative fine motor activity) All of these methods should be demonstrated by the teacher and the *R* sound discussed.

4. *Bells—four or more bells.* (graduated sizes)
Ask what bells do. (ring) Ask what sound *R* makes. Ask if all the "rings" sound the same. Ask each child (one at a time) to ring high, medium or low bell. Leave bells in an area for children to experiment with.

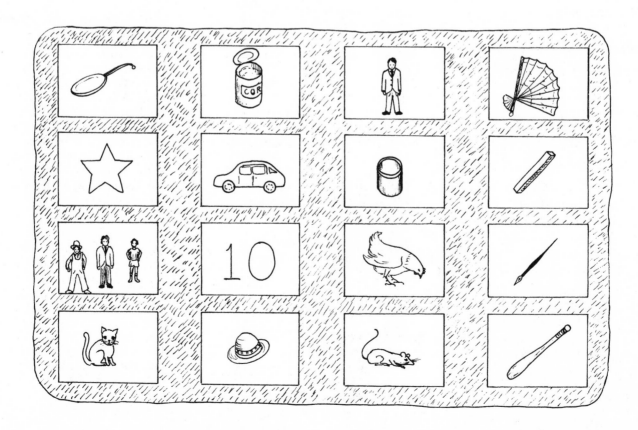

EDUCATIONAL BACKGROUND

Science

In science, preschoolers taste, smell, squeeze, pinch, touch, and hear to check out their perceptions of the world.

Science is exploration, and children are born explorers. They have a drive to explore—watch a crawling baby poking into cabinets, sticking things in her mouth, squishing mud with her fingers, blowing spit bubbles.

Science satisfies the human drive to understand the outer world. Take your children out into the yards, gardens and neighborhoods near your school for science. Study the sky as they experience it, the rain freezing, birds and squirrels. Science materials need not be expensive; they can often be found in your own kitchen, car repair kit, or tool drawer. In science, as in many other areas, you cannot give your children answers; you must help them discover answers for themselves.

Science often includes the best of sensory education. In a trip to the beach, for instance, the children will be involved as total learners: their emotions will soar in the open air, their bodies will move freely in sand and water, their minds can be challenged by the ideas of wet, dry, motion, stillness, hot and cold.

MATERIALS NEEDED

1. Alphabet card
2. Riddle
3. Easel, manila paper, and markers (yellow, blue, brown, black)
4. Sand in a bottle, salt water in a bottle, and coffee stirrers
5. Book—any story about space or spaceships
6. Space puzzle—spaceship, moon, astronaut, or similar object
7. Folder labeled S with pictures of stars, space, sun, sand, spaceships, satellites
8. Floating items (cork, foam, stick), sinking items (stone, nail, buttons, etc.), three tubs (margarine tubs are good), bowl of clear water, labels (sink and float)
9. Books whose titles start with S
10. Trip to sandy beach

ATTENTION GETTER

Nursery Rhymes:
Simple Simon
Sing a Song of Sixpence

ACTIVITIES

1. *Alphabet card.*
   "What letter is this?" Discuss the S sound. "Does anyone's name start with S?" Ask someone to find S on the wall alphabet. "What else starts with the S sound?"

2. *Riddle:*
   It's always here.
   We can't always see it.
   It's hot and it's bright.
   We need it. (Sun)

"Why do we need the sun?"
(caution children about looking
at the sun)

3. *Easel, manila paper, and
markers.*

Fingerplay:

Sun comes up in the morning
(raise hands)
Sun is high above at noon
(clasp hands)
Sun goes down at night
(lower arms)

Have the children repeat the
poem with you.

"Where is the sun?" (out in
space) "Would you like to take
a ride into space?" "How can

we get there?" Draw spaceship.
"What letter does *spaceship*
start with?"

"Let's all put on pretend space
suits." (Go through the motions
of dressing) "Are we ready?
Let's go!" Children should all
crouch down and count—10, 9,
8, 7, 6, 5, 4, 3, 2, 1, BLAST
OFF!

"Now we are up in space. What
do we see?" As children mention stars, moon, sun, satellite,
draw them on the picture.

"It's time to go home. Where
do we land the spaceship?"
Draw the ocean, but mention
that spaceships land on ground

and water. Take off space suits
and sit in circle.

4. *Sand in a bottle, salt water in
a bottle, and stirrers.*
Ask if anyone got water in their
mouth when they landed in the
ocean. "What did it taste like?"
Let the children taste the water
(use stirrers) "What does it taste
like?" "What letter does *salty*
start with?"

Show the bottle of sand. Explain
that the sandy beach is right
next to the ocean. Pour sand in
shallow dish. Ask each child to
feel the sand and describe the
sand.

Special Activity: *Sink and Float*

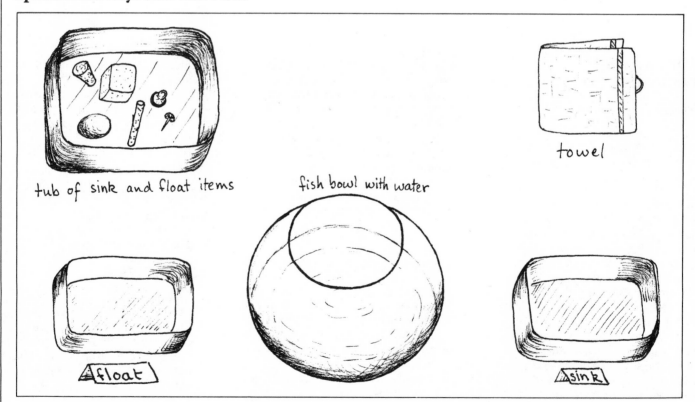

tub of sink and float items

fish bowl with water

towel

float

sink

Materials: Floating items, sinking
items, three tubs, bowl of clear
water, labels (*sink* and *float*)

Discuss words *sink* and *float*. Ask what letter *sink* starts with. Ask
what sound it makes. Ask which word says sink. Demonstrate how
to test items and place in appropriate tub. Dry items before replacing in tub.

"What letter does *sand* start with?" Draw sand.

Name the items in the picture (star, spaceship, satellite, moon, sun). "What is in our picture that does not start with the letter *S*?"

"Do you know a song about something that is in our picture?" Sing: "Twinkle, Twinkle, Little Star"

OPTIONAL FOLLOW-UP ACTIVITIES

1. *Book.*
   Any book about space.

2. *Space puzzle.*

3. *Folder labeled S.*
   Have a folder with pictures of stars, space, sun, sand, spaceships, satellites, etc. for children to look at.

4. *S books.*
   A special corner can be set up for "reading" books whose titles start with the letter *S*. These books can be changed weekly to accommodate the letter being taught.

5. *Take a trip to the beach, a pond or lake, so the children can touch, and talk about the sand.*

"What does the sand feel like when it is dry?" "What does the sand feel like when it is wet?" Discuss how the sand will get dry again.

Other words: *splash, soak, skip,* (children and stones can both skip), *sky.*

Experiment with walking and running in sand: "Don't your feet feel like they're sinking?"

Sand castles: "Can you hear the letter *S* in the middle of the word castle?"

Experience T

EDUCATIONAL BACKGROUND

Body Concept

A child's sense of "me and my importance" is tied to his sense of his own body—its size, its parts, how it works. Children are endlessly interested in themselves and their bodies. Help them form a happy, realistic picture of themselves, and at the same time they can learn about the alphabet.

MATERIALS NEEDED

1. Alphabet card, easel, manila paper, and markers
2. Toaster and bread
3. Play dough, cardboard, or: walnut shell halves, kidney beans, pipe cleaners, glue, black markers
4. Books about trees, drawing or painting supplies
5. Blue construction paper with trunk and branches drawn on it, basket of small leaves

collected by children, glue, scissors, bowl of water, sponge

ATTENTION GETTER

Nursery Rhymes:
One, Two, Buckle My Shoe
Little Tommy Tucker
Tom, Tom, the Piper's Son

ACTIVITIES

1. *Alphabet card, easel, paper, and markers.*
"What letter is this?" Discuss the letter. "Does anyone's name start with *T*?" (If yes, let *T* write it on the easel) "What sound does *T* make?" "What else starts with *T*?" Write words.

Draw two long vertical lines (trunk of tree) "Who knows what these are?" Continue to draw branches and leaves. Ask questions until *tree* is identified. "What letter does *tree* start with?" Write *tree*. "Did you know that trees are like brooms?"

Read poem: *Trees*

Trees grow here and trees grow there
Trees grow almost everywhere.

Trees are short and trees are tall
Trees look pretty in the Fall.

—Lois B. McCue

Draw a shorter tree. "Which is the tallest?" Write *tallest* by tall tree. "Who is the tallest in our circle?" (Have children stand two at a time, back to back, to find out who is the tallest.) "What letter does *tallest* start with?"

Draw a turtle under the tree. "What is this?" "What letter does *turtle* start with?" Write *turtle*. "Who can walk like a turtle?" Allow children to walk around room like turtles.

Read poem: *Tom Tom Turtle*

Tom Tom Turtle
Takes a trip to town

Slowly walking, never talking
As he looks around.

Tom Tom Turtle
Finally got to town
Hello, he said to all his friends
And then he turned around.

Tom Tom Turtle
Had a happy day
Then he fell upon his shell
And there he had to stay.

—Karen J. McCue

(this can be sung to "Row, Row, Row Your Boat")

2. *Toaster and bread.*
"What is this?" Make toast. While the bread is toasting, ask questions. "Can you smell the bread toasting?" "What letter does *toast* start with?" "What sound does *T* make?" "What do you like to put on toast?"

3. *Parts of body.*
"What part of our body starts with the letter *T*?" (toes, teeth, tongue, tummy) "What can we do with our bodies that starts with the letter *T*?" (touch, tiptoe, tickle, tumble, tap, taste) As these movements are expressed, encourage children to act them out. Ask children to tiptoe around the room.

4. *Toast bread.*
Special activity for one to three children.

5. *Turtles.*
Make various kinds of turtles:
(a) play dough
(b) tracing cardboard pattern
(c) walnut shell turtles
Materials needed: walnut shell halves, large kidney beans, pipe cleaners, glue, black marker. Cut pipe cleaner for legs (glue two strips across the underside of the shell with ends extended for feet). Cut smaller pipe cleaner and glue on for tail. Glue kidney bean for head. Use black marker to draw eyes and pattern on turtle's back.

6. *Trees.*
Read a book about trees. Paint or color trees.

SPECIAL ACTIVITY: *Tree*

tree pattern

leaves

scissors   glue

tray

sponge

water

Materials: Blue construction paper with trunk and branches drawn on it, basket of small leaves collected by children, glue, scissors, bowl of water, sponge

Teacher should demonstrate:
(a) cut leaves and glue on branches
(b) use sponge and water to clean up glue that might spill.

Discuss tree and trunk in conjunction with the letter *T*.

Experience U

EDUCATIONAL BACKGROUND

Directionality

Children exploring the world learn the difference between left and right, up and down, over and under, or forward and backward. We help them learn directionality with appropriate activities, like some of the ones in this lesson.

Left to right orientation is important in our culture, because our system of reading is based on left to right directionality. In all classroom activities, work from left to right, to encourage the children's orientation.

MATERIALS NEEDED

1. Alphabet card, flannel board, labels (*U, umbrella, up, under*)
2. Toy umbrella (or party favor umbrella), cloth, tray
3. Pipe cleaners, cupcake papers, (premark dot in center of papers), name tags
4. Up/down picture cards. Examples: star—sand
head—toe
sky—ground
5. Labels—*under, over, around,* etc.
6. Umbrella pattern, pipe cleaners, thin strips of wax paper (rain), pictures of children cut from magazines and catalogues, basket, can, glue, sponge
7. Book—*UMBRELLA* by Tari Yashima

ATTENTION GETTER

Follow the Leader:
Put hands under your head.
Put hands under your chin.
Put hands under your knees.
Put hands under your elbows.
Put hands under your toes.
Put hands under your nose.

ACTIVITIES

1. *Alphabet card, flannel board, labels.*
"What letter is this?" Discuss the letter *U.* "Find the letter *U* on the wall alphabet." Place *U* on flannel board.

2. *Umbrella in tray covered with cloth.*
"I have a surprise under the cloth." "Do you know what letter *under* starts with?" Let children guess and then show them the umbrella. "Do you know what this is?" Place label on flannel board. "What letter does *umbrella* start with?" "What sound does *U* make?"

Relate the following poem to the *U* sound:

The Umbrella

When I was walking down the street
A man with an umbrella I did meet
I said, "Sir, please tell me why
You have an umbrella when the sun's in the sky?"
He said, "Listen to me my good young man,

Listen hard and you'll
  understand!
With my umbrella, I'm all set
For if it rains, I won't get wet."

—Lois B. McCue

3. *Make umbrellas.*
   Materials: pipe cleaners, cupcake papers (dot marked in center) Ask children to follow directions. Poke pipe cleaner through dot, bend over one-quarter inch to keep in place and curve other end for handle.

4. *Up/down picture cards.*
   Classify picture cards. Examples: *star—sand, head—toe*

5. *Obstacle course.*
   Set up an obstacle course where children have to go under some of the obstacles. Label *under, over, around,* etc.

6. *Read book UMBRELLA.*
   Discuss the *U* sound.

SPECIAL ACTIVITY: *Umbrellas*

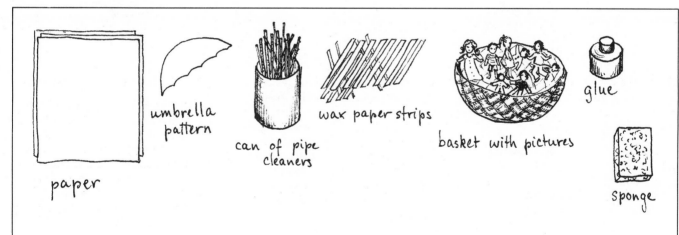

paper

umbrella pattern

can of pipe cleaners

wax paper strips

basket with pictures

glue

sponge

Materials: umbrella pattern, pipe cleaners, thin strips of waxed paper (rain), pictures of children cut from magazines and catalogues, basket, can, glue, sponge

Demonstrate how to glue umbrella pattern and pipe cleaner to make umbrella. Glue boy or girl *under* the umbrella. Glue "rain" on the picture.

Experience V

EDUCATIONAL BACKGROUND

Spatial Relationships

In this lesson, children learn the difference between their own personal space and common space (space shared by everyone). While they are pretend airplanes, they are careful not to crash into other planes. They are learning to move their bodies in and around other people. They practice balance in space. Controlling their bodies helps children manage their world.

MATERIALS NEEDED

1. Alphabet card
2. *STORIES FOR LISTENING: LITTLE VOOM,* Louise B. Scott
3. Markers, 12″ × 18″ manila paper, easel
4. Bag of *V* items: vanilla, vest, vitamins, etc. (same number of items as children), labels
6. Assorted vests
7. Valentine items
8. Vegetable soup–simple or elaborate (dried, canned or from "scratch")
9. Vanilla pudding mix, measuring pitcher, milk, tray, spatula, one-half teaspoon, tablespoon, place mat, wire whip, mixing spoon, bowl, napkins, spoon, towel, detergent, water pitcher, dishpan, sponge, bucket

ATTENTION GETTER

Have pictures of vultures in a folder marked "vultures." Hold up one picture at a time and discuss vultures and their size, habits, and especially the fact that they help to keep the world clean.

ACTIVITIES

1. *Alphabet card.*
   Ask what letter this is. Tell them *vulture* starts with the letter *V*. Ask what sound the letter *V* makes. Show how you can make a *V* with your fingers.

2. *Read the story LITTLE VOOM*

3. *Markers, manila paper, easel.*
   Draw two mountains with a valley in between. Try to get children to identify picture. Point out that *valley* starts with the letter *V*. Ask what sound the letter *V* makes. Draw a vulture in the valley. Discuss and draw Little Voom flying in the valley.

4. *Pretend time* (bag of *V* items and labels)
   Ask children to identify each item as you remove it from the bag. Lay it down on rug and place label on it. Ask what letter each item starts with.

   Draw a store on the picture in the valley. Write *V* on the front of the store. Explain that this store only sells things that start with *V*—the V Store.

   "Now we are going to pretend that we are airplanes that make the 'voom' sound and we are going to the V Store in the valley." Explain that they must be careful not to crash into other planes or into the mountains. Ask children to land their planes; ask them to tell what they bought and what they could do with it.

5. *Trace and cut out Little Voom from a pattern.*
   These could be hung from a wire or string across the room.

6. *Vests.*
   Hang vests in the room that can be worn while children are doing activities. These can be button, zipper, or snap vests.

7. *Valentine activities.*
   Can be incorporated in reinforcing the *V* sound if the holiday is near.

8. *Make vegetable soup as a group.*

SPECIAL ACTIVITY: *Vanilla Pudding*

Materials: Pudding mix, measuring pitcher, milk, tray, spatula, one-half teaspoon, tablespoon, place mat, wire whip, mixing spoon, bowl, napkins, spoon, towel, detergent, water pitcher, dishpan, sponge, bucket

Demonstrate:

(a) Wash hands and put on apron.
(b) Measure one tablespoon and one-half teaspoon pudding mix into bowl (level with spatula).
(c) Measure one-quarter cup milk and pour into bowl; mix with spoon, then beat; pour pudding into dish.
(d) Place napkin on lap and eat pudding.
(e) Put dish and spoon in dishpan.
(f) Wash and dry dishes.
(g) Empty dishwater into bucket.

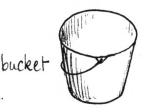

Experience W

EDUCATIONAL BACKGROUND

Water Play

When children wash dolls, wash dishes, or just play in water, tension seems to melt into the water. Water play encourages imagination, independence, coordination, order and concentration.

Rugs

Three foot by five foot (or similar size) rugs in the classroom contribute to order and respect for boundaries. If an activity is confined to a rug, pieces and parts are less likely to be lost. A child can work undisturbed in her space.

MATERIALS NEEDED

1. Alphabet card, manila paper, markers, and wagon
2. Two identical sets of pictures depicting weather and seasons (wind, snow, sunset, etc.) Calendars are a good source for these pictures.
3. Book—*I LIKE WEATHER* by Aileen Fisher (or any book about weather)
4. Instruments (cymbals, sticks, sand blocks, tambourines, and wrist bells)
6. Wagon
7. Walnuts
8. Doll clothes, wash pan, rinse pan, two plastic baskets, pitcher, soap, sponge, bucket

ATTENTION GETTER

Poems:
Wee Willie Winkie
Eensy Weensy Spider

Poem: *Who Has Seen the Wind,* by Christina Rossetti

ACTIVITIES

1. *Alphabet card, paper, markers, and wagon.*
"What letter is this?" Discuss *W.* "Who can find *W* on the wall alphabet?" "Does anyone's name start with *W*?" "What letter does *wagon* start with?" Write *wagon.* "What letter does *walk* start with?" Write *walk.*

"Let's go for a walk with the wagon and see what we can find on our walk." After you return to circle discuss what you found or discovered on the walk. "What kind of weather did we have on our walk?" "What letter does *weather* start with?" Write *weather.*

2. *Two identical sets of pictures.* "These are pictures of different kinds of weather." Lay one set of pictures on a rug. Before you lay down a picture, ask someone to describe the picture. Match one or two from the second set and ask the children to match the remaining pictures.

3. *Book—I LIKE WEATHER.* (or any book about weather)

Tell the name of the book. Discuss the book.

4. *Instruments.*
"Who knows what a thunderstorm is?" Explain that the following poem is about a thunderstorm. Read the poem and demonstrate how to use the instruments.

Poem:
The thunder roars (bang cymbals)
The rain comes down (tap sticks)
  upon our backs (sand blocks)
It shakes the trees (tambourine)
  and frightens birds (wrist bells)
And sounds like many angry words (all instruments)

　　　—Author Unknown

When the poem activity is over, allow unstructured playing of instruments. Explain that a child may not play if he plays too loudly. Have children silence instruments and close eyes. See if they can recognize instruments when played one by one.

OPTIONAL FOLLOW-UP ACTIVITIES

1. *Wagon for free play.*
2. *Perceptual pictures for matching.*
3. *Walnuts to crack and eat.*

SPECIAL ACTIVITY: *Washing doll clothes*

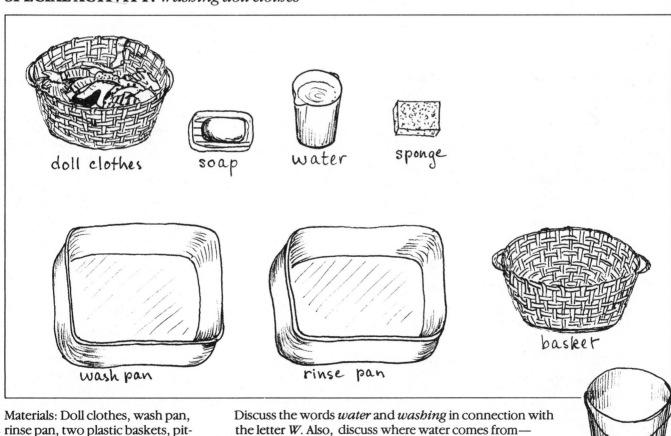

doll clothes　　soap　　water　　sponge

wash pan　　rinse pan　　basket

bucket

Materials: Doll clothes, wash pan, rinse pan, two plastic baskets, pitcher, soap, sponge, bucket

Discuss the words *water* and *washing* in connection with the letter *W*. Also, discuss where water comes from—connect it to the lesson on weather. Hang clothes on line (preferably outside).

Experience X

EDUCATIONAL BACKGROUND

Freedom

Activities that encourage freedom to choose are structured so that the emphasis is placed on learning and not on teaching. Children can choose whether to work alone or in a group. This freedom also makes them responsible for keeping materials in order and the room neat and tidy. Young children are often not allowed the choices of which they are capable. A person can only learn by having the freedom to do for himself, regardless of his age.

MATERIALS NEEDED

1. Alphabet card, *X*, taped in a circle for each child to sit on
2. Cardboard skeleton, book: *THE SKELETON INSIDE YOU,* by Don Bolognese
3. X-rays of bones (these may be obtained from an acquaintance in hospital or physician's office), box, and two labels (*box* and *X-ray*)
4. Records:
   DANCE, SING, AND LISTEN, by the Fifth Dimension, Song: "My Bones"
   GETTING TO KNOW MYSELF, by Hap Palmer
5. Any record, preferably without lyrics
6. Tape *X*'s and *O*'s on the floor
7. Black paper and white paint

ATTENTION GETTER

Touching body parts:
Touch your eyes
Touch your toes
Touch your knees . . .

ACTIVITIES

1. *Alphabet card.*
   "What letter is this?" Ask someone to find *X* on the wall alphabet.

2. *Skeleton.*
   "What is a skeleton?" Encourage questions. Have children identify the skeleton's parts. Book: *THE SKELETON INSIDE YOU,* by Don Bolognese

3. *X-ray films in a box.*
   These can often be obtained through acquaintances in medical professions. Discuss x-rays. Compare the particular bones on x-rays to the skeleton. "What letter does *x-ray* start with?" Show label. Ask children to trace the *X* they are sitting on. Hold up box and label. Point out that *box* ends in the letter X.

4. *Records:*
   "My Bones"—sing and dance
   "Getting to Know Myself"—act out

5. *Ask children to walk on their toe bones around the room.*
   Ask them to come back and stand on an *X*. Play musical "X's" (same as musical chairs). As each child loses an *X*, instead of removing it let him sit on it. This way, she will still be part of the circle.

OPTIONAL FOLLOW-UP ACTIVITIES

1. *Jumping Exercise.*
   Tape X's and O's on the floor.
   Demonstrate that one should only
   jump on the X's.

2. *Black paper and white paint.*
   Demonstrate drawing a skeleton.
   This should be a very simple
   drawing.

Experience Y

EDUCATIONAL BACKGROUND

Food Activities

Young children learn through first hand experiences. Food is part of their world and is an activity that arouses curiosity. Activities which involve food are often social. The skill of using a fork for mashing is a necessary one. Preschool children must practice pouring water, eating, washing a table, and washing and drying dishes. They need practice trying unfamiliar foods.

Food should not be used as a reward in the classroom as much as it should be seen as a learning material that is naturally pleasurable and interesting.

MATERIALS NEEDED

1. Book—*YUMMERS,* by James Marshall
2. Easel, experience paper, black and yellow markers
3. Alphabet card, sandpaper letter
4. Yogurt and spoons
5. *STORIES FOR LISTENING,* by Louise Binder Scott, *THREE LIVELY PUPPIES*
6. Yellow yarn, plastic or cloth shapes, yellow plastic needle
7. Yams, clear pot, butter, place mat, fork, napkin, plate, pitcher, towel, detergent, sponge, bowl, bucket

ATTENTION GETTER

Song: "Yankee Doodle Dandy"

ACTIVITIES

1. *Book—YUMMERS*
   Read and discuss book. "What is a *Yummer?*"

2. *Easel, experience paper, black and yellow markers.*
   Ask each child what his/her favorite *Yummer* is. Write them on the experience paper.

3. *Alphabet card.*
   "What letter is this?" Discuss *Y.* Demonstrate sandpaper letter and have each child take a turn. "*Yum-*

mer starts with *Y.*" If yummers on experience paper have any *Y*'s in them, ask a child to put a yellow circle around one. Continue until all *Y*'s are circled. "What letter does *yellow* start with?" "What is the *Y* sound?" "What letter does *Yankee Doodle* start with?"

4. *Yogurt and spoons.*
   "I'm going to share my yummer with you. This is yogurt. What letter does *yogurt* start with?" Offer a taste to each child.

5. *Ask each child to come up and point to his/her yummer.*
   (This is intentionally done a couple of activities later to develop memory retention.)

6. *STORIES FOR LISTENING,* by Louise Binder Scott *THREE LIVELY PUPPIES*

7. *Sewing with yarn.*
   Demonstrate a simple running or overhand stitch to the edge of the circle, square, etc. Ask what letter *yellow* starts with. Ask what sound

it makes. Repeat with yarn. Place
the exercise on the shelf for
children's independent use.

SPECIAL ACTIVITY: *Yams*

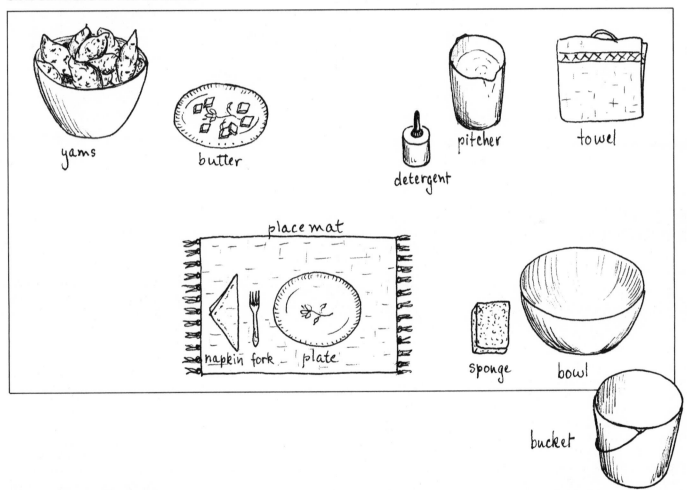

yams

butter

detergent

pitcher

towel

place mat

napkin fork plate

sponge

bowl

bucket

Materials: Yams, clear pot, butter, place mat, fork, napkin, plate, pitcher, towel, detergent, sponge, bowl, bucket

Say, "This is a yam. What does *yam* start with?" Show children that it takes muscle to cut an uncooked yam. Cook yams in a clear pot in the room. (Caution children not to touch the pot—it is hot.) Demonstrate how to peel a yam, mash it, and butter it. Give each child a taste. Discuss the qualities of the cooked yam. Give children time to experiment with mashing.

This could be set up as a special activity or for snack. Cut the yams into single portions, and let each child prepare his own yam for eating.

Experience Z

EDUCATIONAL BACKGROUND

Care of Self

When a child learns to zipper ("What does *zipper* start with?") a vest in the classroom, it is a step towards being independent and self-sufficient. When children wash and dry their own hands, put on their shoes and tie them, snap their pants, buckle their belts, hang up clothes, blow their noses, they can feel proud that they are taking care of themselves. It is important that we allow children to do for themselves—it is their right. We, as teachers, do an injustice when we deprive them of that right.

Maria Montessori states, "Everyone knows that it requires much more time to teach a child how to eat, wash, and clothe himself than it does to

feed, bathe, and clothe him by one-self. The one who does the former is an educator, the latter performs the lower office of a servant."[4]

MATERIALS NEEDED

1. Alphabet card, easel, manila paper, black marker
2. Zebra puzzle or zoo puzzle
3. Any zoo book—be sure that a zebra is in the book
4. Zipper (hidden in a shoe box)
5. Zipper and vest frame
6. Cardboard zebra pattern, paper, markers, pencil, label
7. Zoo and zebra puzzles
8. *STORIES FOR LISTENING,* by Louise Binder Scott, *LITTLE BEE*

ATTENTION GETTER

Make up rhymes: zip, lip, etc. zero, hero, etc. zoo, boo, etc.

ACTIVITIES

1. *Alphabet card, easel, paper, marker.*

"What letter is this?" Write *Z.* Discuss the letter *Z.* "What sound does *Z* make?" "Can you find *Z* on the wall alphabet?"

Draw a zebra on manila paper. As you draw, ask children to guess what you are drawing. "What letter does *zebra* start with?" "What sound does *Z* make?" Write *zebra.* Draw a fence around the zebra. "Where does this zebra live?" "What letter does *zoo* start with?" "What sound does *Z* make?" Write *zoo.*

2. *Zoo puzzle or zebra puzzle.* Take out the puzzle pieces and count them as you lay them on the rug. Encourage children to join in counting. Ask children, one at a time, to help put the puzzle together.

3. *Read book.* Before you begin to read the book, ask the children to zipper their mouths so that everyone can hear the story. Ask what letter *zipper*

[4]Montessori, Maria, *The Discovery of the Child.* Translated by Castellae, M. Joseph, New York. Ballantine Books, 1976.

starts with. ''What sound does a zipper make?''

4. *Zipper.*
Ask children to close their eyes and listen very carefully. Unzip and zip the zipper several times. Ask each child to tell you what he heard. If they cannot guess, allow them to watch you zip and unzip the zipper.

5. *Zipper vest and frame*
Hang vest in the classroom for children to put on and wear. Place frame on shelf for child to practice on.

6. *Zoo or zebra puzzles.*
Place puzzles on the shelf for children's independent use.

7. *STORIES FOR LISTENING,* by Louise B. Scott *LITTLE BEE*

SPECIAL ACTIVITY: *Zebras*

paper

pattern

markers and pencil

zebra

Materials: Cardboard zebra pattern, paper, markers, pencil, label

Demonstrate:
(a) how to trace pattern with black marker
(b) how to put stripes on zebra
(c) how to draw simple grass lines
(d) write zebra on paper
Remember to connect the Z letter and sound with the picture.

Bibliography

FINGERPLAYS

Glazer, Tom. *EYE WINKER, TOM TINKER, CHIN CHOPPER.* Garden City, New York: Doubleday & Company, Inc., 1973.

CHILDREN'S BOOKS

Wade, Harlan. *THE LEVER.* Milwaukee, Wisconsin: Raintree Publishers Limited, 1977.

Fisher, Aileen. I LIKE WEATHER. New York, N.Y.: Thomas Y. Crowell Company, 1963.

Marshall, James. *YUMMERS.* Boston: Houghton Mifflin Company, 1972.

Scott, Louise Binder. *UNFINISHED STORY CARDS.* New York, N.Y.: Webster Division, McGraw-Hill Book Company.

Bronkley, Franklin M. and Vaughn, Eleanor K. *MICKEY'S MAGNET.* New York, N.Y.: Scholastic Book Services, 1956.

RECORDS

Stallman, Lou. *CHILDREN'S DANCES WITHOUT PARTNERS,* THE FINGER GAME. Roslyn Heights, New York: Stallman Educational Systems, Inc.

Jenkins, Ella. *YOU'LL SING A SONG AND I'LL SING A SONG.* New York, N.Y.: Folkways Records FC 7664, 1966.

Scott, Louise Binder. *STORIES FOR LISTENING,* SETS 1, 2, AND 3. New York, N.Y.: Webster Division, McGraw-Hill Book Company, 1970.

RESOURCE BOOKS

Leeper/Dales/Skipper/Witherspoon. *GOOD SCHOOLS FOR YOUNG CHILDREN.* New York: Macmillan Publishing Co., Inc., 1974.

Cromley, Magdalene. *THE YOUNG CHILD, CONNECTING WORDS WITH REAL IDEAS.* Washington, D.C.: NAEYC, Jan. 1978.

Montessori, Maria. *THE ABSORBENT MIND.* New York, N.Y.: Dell Publishing Co., Inc., 1967.

Sisters: Mary Ellen Carinato, Agnes Julia Cluxton, Anne McCarrick, Mary Matz and Marguerite O'Connor. *MONTESSORI MATTERS.* Cincinnati, Ohio: Sisters of Notre Dame de Namur, 1972.

Morrison, George S. *EARLY CHILDHOOD EDUCATION TODAY.* Columbus, Ohio: A Bell & Howell Company, 1980.

Valett, Robert E. *PROGRAMMING LEARNING DISABILITIES.* Belmont, California: Fearon Publishers, Inc., 1968.

Samuels, Shirley C. *ENHANCING SELF-CONCEPT IN EARLY CHILDHOOD.* New York, N.Y.: Human Sciences Press, 1977.

Montessori, Maria. *THE DISCOVERY OF THE CHILD.* Translated by Costellae, M. Joseph, New York, N.Y.: Ballantine Books, 1976.

Copple, Carol; Sigel, Irving E.; and Saunders, Ruth. *EDUCATING THE YOUNG THINKER.* New York, N.Y.: D. Van Nostrand Company.

Caril, Barbara and Richard, Nancy. *ONE PIECE OF THE PUZZLE.* Lumberville, Pennsylvania: Modern Learning Press.

Oren, R.C. *A MONTESSORI HANDBOOK.* New York: Capricorn Books, 1966.

Sharp, Evelyn. *THINKING IS CHILD'S PLAY.* New York: Avon Books, Division of Hearst Corp., 1970.

Hainstock, Elizabeth G. *TEACHING MONTESSORI IN THE HOME.* New York: A Plume Book, New American Library, 1976.

Montessori, Maria. *SPONTANEOUS ACTIVITY IN EDUCATION.* New York, N.Y.: Schocken Books, Inc., 1965.

Glazer, Tom. *DO YOUR EARS HANG LOW?* Garden City, New York: Doubleday and Co., Inc. 1980.

Index